THIRD EDITION

RESUMES FOR

MID-CAREER

JOB CHANGES

With Sample Cover Letters

The Editors of McGraw-Hill

McGraw-Hill

New York   Chicago   San Francisco   Lisbon   London   Madrid   Mexico City
Milan   New Delhi   San Juan   Seoul   Singapore   Sydney   Toronto

Library of Congress Cataloging-in-Publication Data

     Resumes for mid-career job changes : with sample cover letters / the
editors of McGraw-Hill.—3rd ed.
        p.   cm. — (VGM professional resumes series)
    ISBN 0-07-145882-4 (pbk. : alk. paper)
    1. Resumes (Employment)   I. McGraw-Hill Companies.   II. Series

HF5383.R445   2006
650.14′4—dc22   2005053377

1 2 3 4 5 6 7 8 9 0 VLP/VLP 0 9 8 7 6

ISBN 0-07-145882-4

McGraw-Hill books are available at special quantity discounts to use as
premiums and sales promotions, or for use in corporate training programs. For
more information, please write to the Director of Special Sales, Professional
Publishing, McGraw-Hill, Two Penn Plaza, New York, NY 10121-2298. Or contact
your local bookstore.

This book is printed on acid-free paper.

Contents

Introduction

Your resume is a piece of paper (or an electronic document) that serves to introduce you to the people who will eventually hire you. To write a thoughtful resume, you must thoroughly assess your personality, your accomplishments, and the skills you have acquired. The act of composing and submitting a resume also requires you to carefully consider the company or individual that might hire you. What are they looking for, and how can you meet their needs? This book shows you how to organize your personal information and experience into a concise and well-written resume so that your qualifications and potential as an employee will be understood easily and quickly by a complete stranger.

Writing the resume is just one step in what can be a daunting job-search process, but it is an important element in the chain of events that will lead you to your new position. While you are probably a talented, bright, and charming person, your resume may not reflect these qualities. A poorly written resume can get you nowhere; a well-written resume can land you an interview and potentially a job. A good resume can even lead the interviewer to ask you questions that will allow you to talk about your strengths and highlight the skills you can bring to a prospective employer. Even a person with very little experience can find a good job if he or she is assisted by a thoughtful and polished resume.

Lengthy, typewritten resumes are a thing of the past. Today, employers do not have the time or the patience for verbose documents; they look for tightly composed, straightforward, action-based resumes. Although a one-page resume is the norm, a two-page resume may be warranted if you have had extensive job experience or have changed careers and truly need the space to properly position yourself. If, after careful editing, you still need more than one page to present yourself, it's acceptable to use a second page. A crowded resume that's hard to read would be the worst of your choices.

Distilling your work experience, education, and interests into such a small space requires preparation and thought. This book takes you step-by-step through the process of crafting an effective resume that will stand out in today's competitive marketplace. It serves as a workbook and a place to write down your experiences, while also including the techniques you'll need to pull all the necessary elements together. In the following pages, you'll find many examples of resumes that are specific to your area of interest. Study them for inspiration and find what appeals to you. There are a variety of ways to organize and present your information; inside, you'll find several that will be suitable to your needs. Good luck landing the job of your dreams!

Chapter 1

The Elements of an Effective Resume

An effective resume is composed of information that employers are most interested in knowing about a prospective job applicant. This information is conveyed by a few essential elements. The following is a list of elements that are found in most resumes—some essential, some optional. Later in this chapter, we will further examine the role of each of these elements in the makeup of your resume.

- Heading

- Objective and/or Keyword Section

- Work Experience

- Education

- Honors

- Activities

- Certificates and Licenses

- Publications

- Professional Memberships

- Special Skills

- Personal Information

- References

The first step in preparing your resume is to gather information about yourself and your past accomplishments. Later you will refine this information, rewrite it using effective language, and organize it into an attractive layout. But first, let's take a look at each of these important elements individually so you can judge their appropriateness for your resume.

Heading

Although the heading may seem to be the simplest section of your resume, be careful not to take it lightly. It is the first section your prospective employer will see, and it contains the information she or he will need to contact you. At the very least, the heading must contain your name, your home address, and, of course, a phone number where you can be reached easily.

In today's high-tech world, many of us have multiple ways that we can be contacted. You may list your e-mail address if you are reasonably sure the employer makes use of this form of communication. Keep in mind, however, that others may have access to your e-mail messages if you send them from an account provided by your current company. If this is a concern, do not list your work e-mail address on your resume. If you are able to take calls at your current place of business, you should include your work number, because most employers will attempt to contact you during typical business hours.

If you have voice mail or a reliable answering machine at home or at work, list its number in the heading and make sure your greeting is professional and clear. Always include at least one phone number in your heading, even if it is a temporary number, where a prospective employer can leave a message.

You might have a dozen different ways to be contacted, but you do not need to list all of them. Confine your numbers or addresses to those that are the easiest for the prospective employer to use and the simplest for you to retrieve.

Objective

When seeking a specific career path, it is important to list a job or career objective on your resume. This statement helps employers know the direction you see yourself taking, so they can determine whether your goals are in line with those of their organization and the position available. Normally, an objective is one to two sentences long. Its contents will vary depending on your career field, goals, and personality. The objective can be specific or general, but it should always be to the point. See the sample resumes in this book for examples.

If you are planning to use this resume online, or you suspect your potential employer is likely to scan your resume, you will want to include a "keyword" in the objective. This allows a prospective employer, searching hundreds of resumes for a specific skill or position objective, to locate the keyword and find your resume. In essence, a keyword is what's "hot" in your particular field at a given time. It's a buzzword, a shorthand way of getting a particular message across at a glance. For example, if you are a lawyer, your objective might state your desire to work in the area of corporate litigation. In this case, someone searching for the keyword "corporate litigation" will pull up your resume and know that you want to plan, research, and present cases at trial on behalf of the corporation. If your objective states that you "desire a challenging position in systems design," the keyword is "systems design," an industry-specific shorthand way of saying that you want to be involved in assessing the need for, acquiring, and implementing high-technology systems. These are keywords and every industry has them, so it's becoming more and more important to include a few in your resume. (You may need to conduct additional research to make sure you know what keywords are most likely to be used in your desired industry, profession, or situation.)

There are many resume and job-search sites online. Like most things in the online world, they vary a great deal in quality. Use your discretion. If you plan to apply for jobs online or advertise your availability this way, you will want to design a scannable resume. This type of resume uses a format that can be easily scanned into a computer and added to a database. Scanning allows a prospective employer to use keywords to quickly review each applicant's experience and skills, and (in the event that there are many candidates for the job) to keep your resume for future reference.

Many people find that it is worthwhile to create two or more versions of their basic resume. You may want an intricately designed resume on high-quality paper to mail or hand out *and* a resume that is designed to be scanned into a computer and saved on a database or an online job site. You can even create a resume in ASCII text to e-mail to prospective employers. For further information, you may wish to refer to the *Guide to Internet Job Searching*, by Frances Roehm and Margaret Dikel, updated and published every other year by McGraw-Hill. This excellent book contains helpful and detailed information about formatting a resume for Internet use. To get you started, in Chapter 3 we have included a list of things to keep in mind when creating electronic resumes.

Although it is usually a good idea to include an objective, in some cases this element is not necessary. The goal of the objective statement is to provide the employer with an idea of where you see yourself going in the field. However, if you are uncertain of the exact nature of the job you seek, including an objective that is too specific could result in your not being considered for a host of perfectly acceptable positions. If you decide not to use an objective heading in your resume, you should definitely incorporate the information that would be conveyed in the objective into your cover letter.

Work Experience

Work experience is arguably the most important element of them all. Unless you are a recent graduate or former homemaker with little or no relevant work experience, your current and former positions will provide the central focus of the resume. You will want this section to be as complete and carefully constructed as possible. By thoroughly examining your work experience, you can get to the heart of your accomplishments and present them in a way that demonstrates and highlights your qualifications.

If you are just entering the workforce, your resume will probably focus on your education, but you should also include information on your work or volunteer experiences. Although you will have less information about work experience than a person who has held multiple positions or is advanced in his or her career, the amount of information is not what is most important in this section. How the information is presented and what it says about you as a worker and a person are what really count.

As you create this section of your resume, remember the need for accuracy. Include all the necessary information about each of your jobs, including your job title, dates of employment, name of your employer, city, state, responsibilities, special projects you handled, and accomplishments. Be sure to list only accomplishments for which you were directly responsible. And don't be alarmed if you haven't participated in or worked on special projects, because this section may not be relevant to certain jobs.

The most common way to list your work experience is in *reverse chronological order*. In other words, start with your most recent job and work your way backward. This way, your prospective employer sees your current (and often most important) position before considering your past employment. Your most recent position, if it's the most important in terms of responsibilities and relevance to the job for which you are applying, should also be the one that includes the most information as compared to your previous positions.

Even if the work itself seems unrelated to your proposed career path, you should list any job or experience that will help sell your talents. If you were promoted or given greater responsibilities or commendations, be sure to mention the fact.

The following worksheet is provided to help you organize your experiences in the working world. It will also serve as an excellent resource to refer to when updating your resume in the future.

WORK EXPERIENCE

Job One:

Job Title _____

Dates _____

Employer _____

City, State _____

Major Duties _____

_____

_____

_____

_____

_____

_____

_____

Special Projects _____

_____

_____

_____

Accomplishments _____

_____

_____

_____

_____

_____

Job Two:

Job Title _____

Dates _____

Employer _____

City, State _____

Major Duties _____

_____

_____

_____

_____

_____

_____

_____

Special Projects _____

_____

_____

_____

Accomplishments _____

_____

_____

_____

_____

_____

_____

_____

Job Three:

Job Title _____

Dates _____

Employer _____

City, State _____

Major Duties _____

_____

_____

_____

_____

_____

_____

Special Projects _____

_____

_____

_____

Accomplishments _____

_____

_____

_____

_____

_____

_____

_____

_____

Job Four:

Job Title _____

Dates _____

Employer _____

City, State _____

Major Duties _____

_____

_____

_____

_____

_____

_____

_____

Special Projects _____

_____

_____

Accomplishments _____

_____

_____

_____

_____

_____

_____

Education

Education is usually the second most important element of a resume. Your educational background is often a deciding factor in an employer's decision to interview you. Highlight your accomplishments in school as much as you did those accomplishments at work. If you are looking for your first professional job, your education or life experience will be your greatest asset because your related work experience will be minimal. In this case, the education section becomes the most important means of selling yourself.

Include in this section all the degrees or certificates you have received; your major or area of concentration; all of the honors you earned; and any relevant activities you participated in, organized, or chaired. Again, list your most recent schooling first. If you have completed graduate-level work, begin with that and work your way back through your undergraduate education. If you have completed college, you generally should not list your high-school experience; do so only if you earned special honors, you had a grade point average that was much better than the norm, or this was your highest level of education.

If you have completed a large number of credit hours in a subject that may be relevant to the position you are seeking but did not obtain a degree, you may wish to list the hours or classes you completed. Keep in mind, however, that you may be asked to explain why you did not finish the program. If you are currently in school, list the degree, certificate, or license you expect to obtain and the projected date of completion.

The following worksheet will help you gather the information you need for this section of your resume.

EDUCATION

School One _____

Major or Area of Concentration _____

Degree _____

Dates _____

School Two _____

Major or Area of Concentration _____

Degree _____

Dates _____

Honors

If you include an honors section in your resume, you should highlight any awards, honors, or memberships in honorary societies that you have received. (You may also incorporate this information into your education section.) Often, the honors are academic in nature, but this section also may be used for special achievements in sports, clubs, or other school activities. Always include the name of the organization awarding the honor and the date(s) received. Use the following worksheet to help you gather your information.

HONORS

Honor One _____

Awarding Organization _____

Date(s) _____

Honor Two _____

Awarding Organization _____

Date(s) _____

Honor Three _____

Awarding Organization _____

Date(s) _____

Honor Four _____

Awarding Organization _____

Date(s) _____

Honor Five _____

Awarding Organization _____

Date(s) _____

Activities

Perhaps you have been active in different organizations or clubs; often an employer will look at such involvement as evidence of initiative, dedication, and good social skills. Examples of your ability to take a leading role in a group should be included on a resume, if you can provide them. The activities section of your resume should present neighborhood and community activities, volunteer positions, and so forth. In general, you may want to avoid listing any organization whose name indicates the race, creed, sex, age, marital status, sexual orientation, or nation of origin of its members because this could expose you to discrimination. Use the following worksheet to list the specifics of your activities.

ACTIVITIES

Organization/Activity _____

Accomplishments _____

_____

_____

Organization/Activity _____

Accomplishments _____

_____

_____

Organization/Activity _____

Accomplishments _____

_____

_____

As your work experience grows through the years, your school activities and honors will carry less weight and be emphasized less in your resume. Eventually, you will probably list only your degree and any major honors received. As time goes by, your job performance and the experience you've gained become the most important elements in your resume, which should change to reflect this.

Certificates and Licenses

If your chosen career path requires specialized training, you may already have certificates or licenses. You should list these if the job you are seeking requires them and you, of course, have acquired them. If you have applied for a license but have not yet received it, use the phrase "application pending."

License requirements vary by state. If you have moved or are planning to relocate to another state, check with that state's board or licensing agency for all licensing requirements.

Always make sure that all of the information you list is completely accurate. Locate copies of your certificates and licenses, and check the exact date and name of the accrediting agency. Use the following worksheet to organize the necessary information.

CERTIFICATES AND LICENSES

Name of License _____

Licensing Agency _____

Date Issued _____

Name of License _____

Licensing Agency _____

Date Issued _____

Name of License _____

Licensing Agency _____

Date Issued _____

Publications

Some professions strongly encourage or even require that you publish. If you have written, coauthored, or edited any books, articles, professional papers, or works of a similar nature that pertain to your field, you will definitely want to include this element. Remember to list the date of publication and the publisher's name, and specify whether you were the sole author or a coauthor. Book, magazine, or journal titles are generally italicized, while the titles of articles within a larger publication appear in quotes. (Check with your reference librarian for more about the appropriate way to present this information.) For scientific or research papers, you will need to give the date, place, and audience to whom the paper was presented.

Use the following worksheet to help you gather the necessary information about your publications.

PUBLICATIONS

Title and Type (Note, Article, etc.) _____

Title of Publication (Journal, Book, etc.) _____

Publisher _____

Date Published _____

Title and Type (Note, Article, etc.) _____

Title of Publication (Journal, Book, etc.) _____

Publisher _____

Date Published _____

Title and Type (Note, Article, etc.) _____

Title of Publication (Journal, Book, etc.) _____

Publisher _____

Date Published _____

Professional Memberships

Another potential element in your resume is a section listing professional memberships. Use this section to describe your involvement in professional associations, unions, and similar organizations. It is to your advantage to list any professional memberships that pertain to the job you are seeking. Many employers see your membership as representative of your desire to stay up-to-date and connected in your field. Include the dates of your involvement and whether you took part in any special activities or held any offices within the organization. Use the following worksheet to organize your information.

PROFESSIONAL MEMBERSHIPS

Name of Organization _____

Office(s) Held_____

Activities _____

Dates _____

Name of Organization _____

Office(s) Held_____

Activities _____

Dates _____

Name of Organization _____

Office(s) Held_____

Activities _____

Dates _____

Name of Organization _____

Office(s) Held_____

Activities _____

Dates _____

Special Skills

The special skills section of your resume is the place to mention any special abilities you have that relate to the job you are seeking. You can use this element to present certain talents or experiences that are not necessarily a part of your education or work experience. Common examples include fluency in a foreign language, extensive travel abroad, or knowledge of a particular computer application. "Special skills" can encompass a wide range of talents, and this section can be used creatively. However, for each skill you list, you should be able to describe how it would be a direct asset in the type of work you're seeking because employers may ask just that in an interview. If you can't think of a way to do this, it may be extraneous information.

Personal Information

Some people include personal information on their resumes. This is generally not recommended, but you might wish to include it if you think that something in your personal life, such as a hobby or talent, has some bearing on the position you are seeking. This type of information is often referred to at the beginning of an interview, when it may be used as an icebreaker. Of course, personal information regarding your age, marital status, race, religion, or sexual orientation should never appear on your resume as personal information. It should be given only in the context of memberships and activities, and only when doing so would not expose you to discrimination.

References

References are not usually given on the resume itself, but a prospective employer needs to know that you have references who may be contacted if necessary. All you need to include is a single sentence at the end of the resume: "References are available upon request," or even simply, "References available." Have a reference list ready—your interviewer may ask to see it! Contact each person on the list ahead of time to see whether it is all right for you to use him or her as a reference. This way, the person has a chance to think about what to say *before* the call occurs. This helps ensure that you will obtain the best reference possible.

Chapter 2

Writing Your Resume

Now that you have gathered the information for each section of your resume, it's time to write it out in a way that will get the attention of the reviewer—hopefully, your future employer! The language you use in your resume will affect its success, so you must be careful and conscientious. Translate the facts you have gathered into the active, precise language of resume writing. You will be aiming for a resume that keeps the reader's interest and highlights your accomplishments in a concise and effective way.

Resume writing is unlike any other form of writing. Although your seventh-grade composition teacher would not approve, the rules of punctuation and sentence building are often completely ignored. Instead, you should try for a functional, direct writing style that focuses on the use of verbs and other words that imply action on your part. Writing with action words and strong verbs characterizes you to potential employers as an energetic, active person, someone who completes tasks and achieves results from his or her work. Resumes that do not make use of action words can sound passive and stale. These resumes are not effective and do not get the attention of any employer, no matter how qualified the applicant. Choose words that display your strengths and demonstrate your initiative. The following list of commonly used verbs will help you create a strong resume:

administered	assembled
advised	assumed responsibility
analyzed	billed
arranged	built

carried out	inspected
channeled	interviewed
collected	introduced
communicated	invented
compiled	maintained
completed	managed
conducted	met with
contacted	motivated
contracted	negotiated
coordinated	operated
counseled	orchestrated
created	ordered
cut	organized
designed	oversaw
determined	performed
developed	planned
directed	prepared
dispatched	presented
distributed	produced
documented	programmed
edited	published
established	purchased
expanded	recommended
functioned as	recorded
gathered	reduced
handled	referred
hired	represented
implemented	researched
improved	reviewed

saved	supervised
screened	taught
served as	tested
served on	trained
sold	typed
suggested	wrote

Let's look at two examples that differ only in their writing style. The first resume section is ineffective because it does not use action words to accent the applicant's work experiences.

WORK EXPERIENCE
Regional Sales Manager

Manager of sales representatives from seven states. Manager of twelve food chain accounts in the East. In charge of the sales force's planned selling toward specific goals. Supervisor and trainer of new sales representatives. Consulting for customers in the areas of inventory management and quality control.

Special Projects: Coordinator and sponsor of annual Food Industry Seminar.

Accomplishments: Monthly regional volume went up 25 percent during my tenure while, at the same time, a proper sales/cost ratio was maintained. Customer-company relations were improved.

In the following paragraph, we have rewritten the same section using action words. Notice how the tone has changed. It now sounds stronger and more active. This person accomplished goals and really *did* things.

WORK EXPERIENCE
Regional Sales Manager

Managed sales representatives from seven states. Oversaw twelve food chain accounts in the eastern United States. Directed the sales force in planned selling toward specific goals. Supervised and trained new sales representatives. Counseled customers in the areas of inventory management and quality control. Coordinated and sponsored the annual Food Industry Seminar. Increased monthly regional volume by 25 percent and helped to improve customer-company relations during my tenure.

One helpful way to construct the work experience section is to make use of your actual job descriptions—the written duties and expectations your employers have for a person in your current or former position. Job descriptions are rarely written in proper resume language, so you will have to rework them, but they do include much of the information necessary to create this section of your resume. If you have access to job descriptions for your former positions, you can use the details to construct an action-oriented paragraph. Often, your human resources department can provide a job description for your current position.

The following is an example of a typical human resources job description, followed by a rewritten version of the same description employing action words and specific details about the job. Again, pay attention to the style of writing instead of the content, as the details of your own experience will be unique.

WORK EXPERIENCE
Public Administrator I

Responsibilities: Coordinate and direct public services to meet the needs of the nation, state, or community. Analyze problems; work with special committees and public agencies; recommend solutions to governing bodies.

Aptitudes and Skills: Ability to relate to and communicate with people; solve complex problems through analysis; plan, organize, and implement policies and programs. Knowledge of political systems, financial management, personnel administration, program evaluation, and organizational theory.

WORK EXPERIENCE
Public Administrator I

Wrote pamphlets and conducted discussion groups to inform citizens of legislative processes and consumer issues. Organized and supervised 25 interviewers. Trained interviewers in effective communication skills.

After you have written out your resume, you are ready to begin the next important step: assembly and layout.

Chapter 3

Assembly and Layout

A t this point, you've gathered all the necessary information for your resume and rewritten it in language that will impress your potential employers. Your next step is to assemble the sections in a logical order and lay them out on the page neatly and attractively to achieve the desired effect: getting the interview.

Assembly

The order of the elements in a resume makes a difference in its overall effect. Clearly, you would not want to bury your name and address somewhere in the middle of the resume. Nor would you want to lead with a less important section, such as special skills. Put the elements in an order that stresses your most important accomplishments and the things that will be most appealing to your potential employer. For example, if you are new to the workforce, you will want the reviewer to read about your education and life skills before any part-time jobs you may have held for short durations. On the other hand, if you have been gainfully employed for several years and currently hold an important position in your company, you should list your work accomplishments ahead of your educational information, which has become less pertinent with time.

Certain things should always be included in your resume, but others are optional. The following list shows you which are which. You might want to use it as a checklist to be certain that you have included all of the necessary information.

Essential	**Optional**
Name	Cellular Phone Number
Address	Pager Number
Phone Number	E-Mail Address or Website Address
Work Experience	Voice Mail Number
Education	Job Objective
References Phrase	Honors
	Special Skills
	Publications
	Professional Memberships
	Activities
	Certificates and Licenses
	Personal Information
	Graphics
	Photograph

Your choice of optional sections depends on your own background and employment needs. Always use information that will put you in a favorable light—unless it's absolutely essential, avoid anything that will prompt the interviewer to ask questions about your weaknesses or something else that could be unflattering. Make sure your information is accurate and truthful. If your honors are impressive, include them in the resume. If your activities in school demonstrate talents that are necessary for the job you are seeking, allow space for a section on activities. If you are applying for a position that requires ornamental illustration, you may want to include border illustrations or graphics that demonstrate your talents in this area. If you are answering an advertisement for a job that requires certain physical traits, a photo of yourself might be appropriate. A person applying for a job as a computer programmer would *not* include a photo as part of his or her resume. Each resume is unique, just as each person is unique.

Types of Resumes

So far we have focused on the most common type of resume—the *reverse chronological* resume—in which your most recent job is listed first. This is the type of resume usually preferred by those who have to read a large number of resumes, and it is by far the most popular and widely circulated. However, this style of presentation may not be the most effective way to highlight *your* skills and accomplishments.

For example, if you are reentering the workforce after many years or are trying to change career fields, the *functional* resume may work best. This type of resume puts the focus on your achievements instead of the sequence of your work history. In the functional resume, your experience is presented through your general accomplishments and the skills you have developed in your working life.

A functional resume is assembled from the same information you gathered in Chapter 1. The main difference lies in how you organize the information. Essentially, the work experience section is divided in two, with your job duties and accomplishments constituting one section and your employers' names, cities, and states; your positions; and the dates employed making up the other. Place the first section near the top of your resume, just below your job objective (if used), and call it *Accomplishments* or *Achievements*. The second section, containing the bare essentials of your work history, should come after the accomplishments section and can be called *Employment History*, since it is a chronological overview of your former jobs.

The other sections of your resume remain the same. The work experience section is the only one affected in the functional format. By placing the section that focuses on your achievements at the beginning, you draw attention to these achievements. This puts less emphasis on where you worked and when, and more on what you did and what you are capable of doing.

If you are changing careers, the emphasis on skills and achievements is important. The identities of previous employers (who aren't part of your new career field) need to be downplayed. A functional resume can help accomplish this task. If you are reentering the workforce after a long absence, a functional resume is the obvious choice. And if you lack full-time work experience, you will need to draw attention away from this fact and put the focus on your skills and abilities. You may need to highlight your volunteer activities and part-time work. Education may also play a more important role in your resume.

The type of resume that is right for you will depend on your personal circumstances. It may be helpful to create both types and then compare them. Which one presents you in the best light? Examples of both types of resumes are included in this book. Use the sample resumes in Chapter 5 to help you decide on the content, presentation, and look of your own resume.

Resume or Curriculum Vitae?

A curriculum vitae (CV) is a longer, more detailed synopsis of your professional history, which generally runs three or more pages in length. It includes a summary of your educational and academic background as well as teaching and research experience, publications, presentations, awards, honors, affiliations, and other details. Because the purpose of the CV is different from that of the resume, many of the rules we've discussed thus far involving style and length do not apply.

A curriculum vitae is used primarily for admissions applications to graduate or professional schools, independent consulting in a variety of settings, proposals for fellowships or grants, or applications for positions in academia. As with a resume, you may need different versions of a CV for different types of positions. You should only send a CV when one is specifically requested by an employer or institution.

Like a resume, your CV should include your name, contact information, education, skills, and experience. In addition to the basics, a CV includes research and teaching experience, publications, grants and fellowships, professional associations and licenses, awards, and other information relevant to the position for which you are applying. You can follow the advice presented thus far to gather and organize your personal information.

Special Tips for Electronic Resumes

Because there are many details to consider in writing a resume that will be posted or transmitted on the Internet, or one that will be scanned into a computer when it is received, we suggest that you refer to the *Guide to Internet Job Searching*, by Frances Roehm and Margaret Dikel, as previously mentioned. However, here are some brief, general guidelines to follow if you expect your resume to be scanned into a computer.

- Use standard fonts in which none of the letters touch.

- Keep in mind that underlining, italics, and fancy scripts may not scan well.

- Use boldface and capitalization to set off elements. Again, make sure letters don't touch. Leave at least a quarter inch between lines of type.

- Keep information and elements at the left margin. Centering, columns, and even indenting may change when the resume is optically scanned.

- Do not use any lines, boxes, or graphics.

- Place the most important information at the top of the first page. If you use two pages, put "Page 1 of 2" at the bottom of the first page and put your name and "Page 2 of 2" at the top of the second page.

- List each telephone number on its own line in the header.

- Use multiple keywords or synonyms for what you do to make sure your qualifications will be picked up if a prospective employer is searching for them. Use nouns that are keywords for your profession.

- Be descriptive in your titles. For example, don't just use "assistant"; use "legal office assistant."

- Make sure the contrast between print and paper is good. Use a high-quality laser printer and white or very light colored 8½-by-11-inch paper.

- Mail a high-quality laser print or an excellent copy. Do not fold or use staples, as this might interfere with scanning. You may, however, use paper clips.

In addition to creating a resume that works well for scanning, you may want to have a resume that can be e-mailed to reviewers. Because you may not know what word processing application the recipient uses, the best format to use is ASCII text. (ASCII stands for "American Standard Code for Information Interchange.") It allows people with very different software platforms to exchange and understand information. (E-mail operates on this principle.) ASCII is a simple, text-only language, which means you can include only simple text. There can be no use of boldface, italics, or even paragraph indentations.

To create an ASCII resume, just use your normal word processing program; when finished, save it as a "text only" document. You will find this option under the "save" or "save as" command. Here is a list of things to *avoid* when crafting your electronic resume:

- Tabs. Use your space bar. Tabs will not work.

- Any special characters, such as mathematical symbols.

- Word wrap. Use hard returns (the return key) to make line breaks.

- Centering or other formatting. Align everything at the left margin.

- Bold or italic fonts. Everything will be converted to plain text when you save the file as a "text only" document.

Check carefully for any mistakes before you save the document as a text file. Spellcheck and proofread it several times; then ask someone with a keen eye to go over it again for you. Remember: the key is to keep it simple. Any attempt to make this resume pretty or decorative may result in a resume that is confusing and hard to read. After you have saved the document, you can cut and paste it into an e-mail or onto a website.

Layout for a Paper Resume

A great deal of care—and much more formatting—is necessary to achieve an attractive layout for your paper resume. There is no single appropriate layout that applies to every resume, but there are a few basic rules to follow in putting your resume on paper:

- Leave a comfortable margin on the sides, top, and bottom of the page (usually one to one and a half inches).

- Use appropriate spacing between the sections (two to three line spaces are usually adequate).

- Be consistent in the *type* of headings you use for different sections of your resume. For example, if you capitalize the heading EMPLOY-MENT HISTORY, don't use initial capitals and underlining for a section of equal importance, such as Education.

- Do not use more than one font in your resume. Stay consistent by choosing a font that is fairly standard and easy to read, and don't change it for different sections. Beware of the tendency to try to make your resume original by choosing fancy type styles; your resume may end up looking unprofessional instead of creative. Unless you are in a very creative and artistic field, you should almost always stick with tried-and-true type styles like Times New Roman and Palatino, which are often used in business writing. In the area of resume styles, conservative is usually the best way to go.

CHRONOLOGICAL RESUME

Franklin Wu
5391 Southward Plaza
Walnut Creek, CA 94596
(510) 555-9008

JOB OBJECTIVE:

To obtain a position as a management optician in a fast-paced retail store.

EDUCATION:

Graduated Hayward Community College, Hayward, CA in June of 1991
Graduated North Central High School, Chicago, IL in June of 1989

WORK EXPERIENCE:

1995 - present

Great Spectacles, Walnut Creek, CA
Management Optician

Valley Vision, Pleasanton, CA
Management Optician and Frame Buyer

SPECIAL SKILLS:

People person; fashion styling experience; knowledge of adjustments, repairs, and fittings of glasses and contact lenses.

CERTIFICATION:

American Board of Optometry Certificate

SEMINARS:

Cal-Q Optics to prepare for licensing, 1997
Opti-Fair (annual, three-day seminars)

REFERENCES:

George Jones, O.D.
Great Spectacles, (510) 555-8941

Maria Lazar, Optician
Valley Vision, (510) 555-3726

FUNCTIONAL RESUME

PATRICIA WHITE
987 West 44th Street
Cheyenne, WY 82001
(307) 555-9872

PROFESSIONAL OBJECTIVE

Opportunity to demonstrate superior managerial ability and administrative decision-making skills in a nursing home environment.

SUMMARY OF QUALIFICATIONS

- High degree of motivation
- Ability and patience to train and develop office and professional staff
- Thorough knowledge of IBM PC, Lotus 1-2-3, WordPerfect, IBM 38
- 10-key by touch
- Dictation

EDUCATION

University of Wyoming, B.A. Business
Laramie, WY

EXPERIENCE

1994 to Present - Assistant Director, Longview Manor, Cheyenne, WY
1991 to 1994 - Business Manager, Mountain Top Nursing Home, Cheyenne, WY

REFERENCES

Excellent professional and personal references

- Always try to fit your resume on one page. If you are having trouble with this, you may be trying to say too much. Edit out any repetitive or unnecessary information, and shorten descriptions of earlier jobs where possible. Ask a friend you trust for feedback on what seems unnecessary or unimportant. For example, you may have included too many optional sections. Today, with the prevalence of the personal computer as a tool, there is no excuse for a poorly laid out resume. Experiment with variations until you are pleased with the result.

Remember that a resume is not an autobiography. Too much information will only get in the way. The more compact your resume, the easier it will be to review. If a person who is swamped with resumes looks at yours, catches the main points, and then calls you for an interview to fill in some of the details, your resume has already accomplished its task. A clear and concise resume makes for a happy reader and a good impression.

There are times when, despite extensive editing, the resume simply cannot fit on one page. In this case, the resume should be laid out on two pages in such a way that neither clarity nor appearance is compromised. Each page of a two-page resume should be marked clearly: the first should indicate "Page 1 of 2," and the second should include your name and the page number, for example, "Julia Ramirez—Page 2 of 2." The pages should then be paper-clipped together. You may use a smaller type size (in the same font as the body of your resume) for the page numbers. Place them at the bottom of page one and the top of page two. Again, spend the time now to experiment with the layout until you find one that looks good to you.

Always show your final layout to other people and ask them what they like or dislike about it, and what impresses them most when they read your resume. Make sure that their responses are the same as what you want to elicit from your prospective employer. If they aren't the same, you should continue to make changes until the necessary information is emphasized.

Proofreading

After you have finished typing the master copy of your resume and before you have it copied or printed, thoroughly check it for typing and spelling errors. Do not place all your trust in your computer's spellcheck function. Use an old editing trick and read the whole resume backward—start at the end and read it right to left and bottom to top. This can help you see the small errors or inconsistencies that are easy to overlook. Take time to do it right because a single error on a document this important can cause the reader to judge your attention to detail in a harsh light.

Have several people look at the finished resume just in case you've missed an error. Don't try to take a shortcut; not having an unbiased set of eyes examine your resume now could mean embarrassment later. Even experienced editors can easily overlook their own errors. Be thorough and conscientious with your proofreading so your first impression is a perfect one.

We have included the following rules of capitalization and punctuation to assist you in the final stage of creating your resume. Remember that resumes often require use of a shorthand style of writing that may include sentences without periods and other stylistic choices that break the standard rules of grammar. Be consistent in each section and throughout the whole resume with your choices.

RULES OF CAPITALIZATION

- Capitalize proper nouns, such as names of schools, colleges, and universities; names of companies; and brand names of products.

- Capitalize major words in the names and titles of books, tests, and articles that appear in the body of your resume.

- Capitalize words in major section headings of your resume.

- Do not capitalize words just because they seem important.

- When in doubt, consult a style manual such as *Words into Type* (Prentice Hall) or *The Chicago Manual of Style* (The University of Chicago Press). Your local library can help you locate these and other reference books. Many computer programs also have grammar help sections.

RULES OF PUNCTUATION

- Use commas to separate words in a series.

- Use a semicolon to separate series of words that already include commas within the series. (For an example, see the first rule of capitalization.)

- Use a semicolon to separate independent clauses that are not joined by a conjunction.

- Use a period to end a sentence.

- Use a colon to show that examples or details follow that will expand or amplify the preceding phrase.

- Avoid the use of dashes.

- Avoid the use of brackets.

- If you use any punctuation in an unusual way in your resume, be consistent in its use.

- Whenever you are uncertain, consult a style manual.

Putting Your Resume in Print

You will need to buy high-quality paper for your printer before you print your finished resume. Regular office paper is not good enough for resumes; the reviewer will probably think it looks flimsy and cheap. Go to an office supply store or copy shop and select a high-quality bond paper that will make a good first impression. Select colors like white, off-white, or possibly a light gray. In some industries, a pastel may be acceptable, but be sure the color and feel of the paper make a subtle, positive statement about you. Nothing in the choice of paper should be loud or unprofessional.

If your computer printer does not reproduce your resume properly and produces smudged or stuttered type, either ask to borrow a friend's or take your disk (or a clean original) to a printer or copy shop for high-quality copying. If you anticipate needing a large number of copies, taking your resume to a copy shop or a printer is probably the best choice.

Hold a sheet of your unprinted bond paper up to the light. If it has a watermark, you will want to point this out to the person helping you with copies; the printing should be done so that the reader can read the print and see the watermark the right way up. Check each copy for smudges or streaks. This is the time to be a perfectionist—the results of your careful preparation will be well worth it.

The Cover Letter

Once your resume has been assembled, laid out, and printed to your satisfaction, the next and final step before distribution is to write your cover letter. Though there may be instances where you deliver your resume in person, you will usually send it through the mail or online. Resumes sent through the mail always need an accompanying letter that briefly introduces you and your resume. The purpose of the cover letter is to get a potential employer to read your resume, just as the purpose of the resume is to get that same potential employer to call you for an interview.

Like your resume, your cover letter should be clean, neat, and direct. A cover letter usually includes the following information:

1. Your name and address (unless it already appears on your personal letterhead) and your phone number(s); see item 7.

2. The date.

3. The name and address of the person and company to whom you are sending your resume.

4. The salutation ("Dear Mr." or "Dear Ms." followed by the person's last name, or "To Whom It May Concern" if you are answering a blind ad).

5. An opening paragraph explaining why you are writing (for example, in response to an ad, as a follow-up to a previous meeting, at the suggestion of someone you both know) and indicating that you are interested in whatever job is being offered.

6. One or more paragraphs that tell why you want to work for the company and what qualifications and experiences you can bring to the position. This is a good place to mention some detail about

that particular company that makes you want to work for them; this shows that you have done some research before applying.

7. A final paragraph that closes the letter and invites the reviewer to contact you for an interview. This can be a good place to tell the potential employer which method would be best to use when contacting you. Be sure to give the correct phone number and a good time to reach you, if that is important. You may mention here that your references are available upon request.

8. The closing ("Sincerely" or "Yours truly") followed by your signature in a dark ink, with your name typed under it.

Your cover letter should include all of this information and be no longer than one page in length. The language used should be polite, businesslike, and to the point. Don't attempt to tell your life story in the cover letter; a long and cluttered letter will serve only to annoy the reader. Remember that you need to mention only a few of your accomplishments and skills in the cover letter. The rest of your information is available in your resume. If your cover letter is a success, your resume will be read and all pertinent information reviewed by your prospective employer.

Producing the Cover Letter

Cover letters should always be individualized because they are always written to specific individuals and companies. Never use a form letter for your cover letter or copy it as you would a resume. Each cover letter should be unique, and as personal and lively as possible. (Of course, once you have written and rewritten your first cover letter until you are satisfied with it, you can certainly use similar wording in subsequent letters. You may want to save a template on your computer for future reference.) Keep a hard copy of each cover letter so you know exactly what you wrote in each one.

There are sample cover letters in Chapter 6. Use them as models or for ideas of how to assemble and lay out your own cover letters. Remember that every letter is unique and depends on the particular circumstances of the individual writing it and the job for which he or she is applying.

After you have written your cover letter, proofread it as thoroughly as you did your resume. Again, spelling or punctuation errors are a sure sign of carelessness, and you don't want that to be a part of your first impression on a prospective employer. This is no time to trust your spellcheck function. Even after going through a spelling and grammar check, your cover letter should be carefully proofread by at least one other person.

Print the cover letter on the same quality bond paper you used for your resume. Remember to sign it, using a good dark-ink pen. Handle the letter and resume carefully to avoid smudging or wrinkling, and mail them together in an appropriately sized envelope. Many stores sell matching envelopes to coordinate with your choice of bond paper.

Keep an accurate record of all resumes you send out and the results of each mailing. This record can be kept on your computer, in a calendar or notebook, or on file cards. Knowing when a resume is likely to have been received will keep you on track as you make follow-up phone calls.

About a week after mailing resumes and cover letters to potential employers, contact them by telephone. Confirm that your resume arrived and ask whether an interview might be possible. Be sure to record the name of the person you spoke to and any other information you gleaned from the conversation. It is wise to treat the person answering the phone with a great deal of respect; sometimes the assistant or receptionist has the ear of the person doing the hiring.

You should make a great impression with the strong, straightforward resume and personalized cover letter you have just created. We wish you every success in securing the career of your dreams!

Chapter 5

Sample Resumes

This chapter contains dozens of sample resumes for people pursuing a wide variety of jobs and careers.

There are many different styles of resumes in terms of graphic layout and presentation of information. These samples represent people with varying amounts of education and experience. Use them as models for your own resume. Choose one resume or borrow elements from several different resumes to help you construct your own.

SHARYL WILSON
84 Saratoga Avenue • Detroit, MI 48229
(313) 555-9388 • sharyl-wilson@xxx.com

SUMMARY

Sales and Marketing Manager with proven ability to conceptualize, structure, and achieve both market and profit objectives seeks to join the sales and marketing team of Fortune 500 manufacturer.

Sales

- Initiated sales incentive program to motivate the sales force to generate new product sales.
- Increased sales of recycled paper products from $250,000 to $600,000 in the first year. Successfully built sales to more than $3,000,000 over the next five years.
- Held total responsibility for sales of copy-type papers, which represented 40 percent of total sales volume.
- Supervised six sales professionals.
- Initiated aggressive sales efforts for additional volume, allowing increased production using idle equipment, which spread costs and substantially improved profits.
- Successful in developing new corporate accounts.

Management and Marketing

- Spearheaded new Web marketing strategy leading to 28 percent increase in Web sales.
- Created and implemented the Neighborhood Business Strategy concentrating sales efforts to develop business close to the mill, effectively reducing costs and improving profitability.
- Changed company image from volume supplier to a dedicated quality product producer and provider of top-level customer service, a strategy that enhanced repeat business.
- Assumed newly created position, established its purpose, and made it work profitably.
- Established specifications, pricing, and developed marketing strategies for Web, print, and television.
- Implemented multimedia advertising campaigns with assistance from ad agencies.

EMPLOYMENT EXPERIENCE

National Sales Manager, Starnes Paper, Subsidiary of Weyerhauser, Inc.
Detroit, MI, 2004–present

Regional Sales Manager, James River, Inc.
Grand Rapids, MI, 1995–2004

Regional Sales Manager, Specialty Papers, Greenfield Paper Company, Subsidiary
of James River, Inc.
Grand Rapids, MI, 1992–1995

Sales Manager, Greenfield Paper Company
Grand Rapids, MI, 1983–1992

EDUCATION

M.B.A., Harvard University, Cambridge, MA, 1983
B.S., Business and Economics, University of California, Berkeley, 1981

REFERENCES AVAILABLE UPON REQUEST

Tanya Stewart

325 Matney Street
West Village, Utah 84872
(801) 555-7151
tanyastewart@xxx.com

Career Objective

To bring my extensive communications background to the public relations department of a mid-sized West Coast computer company.

Related Skills and Experience

- Developed and produced a prototype newsletter to be distributed among alumni of the College of Science at Brigham Young University.
- Conducted reader survey to determine market interest and gather information relevant to the publication. Supervised continued publication of the newsletter.
- Responded to queries from readers.
- Conducted seminars on publication writing for scientists and other technical professionals.
- Designed and instituted online courses in technical writing and communication for science and engineering majors.
- Managed all institutional correspondence and communication with the news media.
- Worked closely with public relations office of the university in developing news stories about scientific work conducted by university faculty in my college.
- Widely published in scientific and technical journals. Published two textbooks on scientific method in computer-aided investigation.
- Worked with science correspondents of major medical journals on the reporting of significant developments in cancer research at a medical laboratory under my direct supervision.

Employment

Brigham Young University, Provo, Utah
• Associate Dean, College of Science, 2005 to present
• Professor of Science, 2000 to present
• Associate Professor, 1997 to 2000
• Assistant Professor, 1994 to 1997

Mentor Laboratories, Salt Lake City, Utah
• Director of Research, 1989 to 1994
• Research Scientist, 1985 to 1989

Education

Bethlehem Children's Hospital, Pleasantville, Maryland
• Postdoctoral Fellow, Cancer Research Unit, 1992 to 1994

University of Wisconsin, Milwaukee
• Doctorate, Chemistry, 1988

University of Miami, Florida
• Bachelor of Science, Chemistry, 1985

Publications list and references are available on request.

DARIUS W. HARMS

3485 Plainfield Road

Lincoln, Nebraska 68573

(402) 555-9287

dariusharms@xxx.com

CAREER GOAL

A position in engineering management in the public sector

ACHIEVEMENTS & EXPERIENCE

- Supported construction and operating personnel during installation, start-up, and testing of propulsion generator and hydraulic machinery.
- Performed facility survey, prepared technical reports, and provided engineering support during construction, start-up, and testing of the propulsion turbine plant.
- Directed structural and mechanical equipment development and operations.
- Coordinated fabrication and installation of full-size mock-up for integrated sub-base turbo generator.
- Provided support to designers, draftsmen, and construction personnel to ensure compliance with technical specifications and code requirements.
- Designed various mechanical and fluid systems and assisted in procurement, installation, and testing of systems and equipment.
- Designed and assisted in construction and testing of a flow-through crude-oil handling system on oil recycler, reducing initial cost and increasing operational efficiency.
- Conducted equipment and system test at the factory and after-site installation of various recycling components, including pumps, heat exchangers, hydraulics, and control/monitoring devices.
- Assisted in installation and testing of bulk petrochemical heating system.
- Assisted during installation, start-up, and testing of machinery for fiber, film cellulose, bulk material, and processing equipment.
- Developed and assisted in installation of automated overhead conveying system to replace manual material handling operation for cellulose sheet.
- Supervised installation of the filing line to increase bagging output for micro crystalline cellulose.

ACHIEVEMENTS & EXPERIENCE (CONTINUED)

- Redesigned the PVC blown film machine and provided assistance during installation and start-up.
- Supervised a workforce of 120 with responsibility over production and maintenance of oxygen and acetylene plant and facilities.
- Conducted the economic analysis for relocating oxygen plant.
- Supervised erection of the plant at the new site.
- Designed and assisted in the fabrication of the filtering system for acetylene. Supervised start-up and testing of the system.
- Developed the test procedure for high pressure cylinders to meet regulatory requirements.

WORK HISTORY

2005–Present
Benton Recycling Machinery, Inc., Lincoln, Nebraska
Senior Engineer

1994–2005
Taber Manufacturing, Lincoln, Nebraska
Engineering Supervisor

1980–1989
Tutwiller Bond Oxygen Corp., Ltd., Topeka, Kansas
Staff Engineer, Maintenance Engineer, Technician

EDUCATION

1986
M.S., Mechanical Engineering
University of Kansas

1980
B.S., Mechanical Engineering
University of Nebraska–Lincoln

References on Request

Judd Riley, Jr.

P.O. Box 1254 • Sioux Falls, SD 57103 • (605) 555-3828 • juddriley@xxx.com

Job Objective
Customer Service Department managerial position

Experience & Achievements
Public Relations (current)
❖ Direct interaction with clients and the public.
❖ Assess needs and provide solutions to customer complaints.
❖ Assist in product inquiries and setting up discounting programs for qualified customers.
❖ Represent company at trade shows.
❖ Utilize strong product knowledge in handling customer complaints through analysis and evaluation of complaint report.
❖ Support for sales force and on-site technicians.

Sales & Marketing (previous)
❖ Assisted marketing research projects and conducted a general management survey for mini-warehouse industry.
❖ Coordinated promotional campaigns, utilizing database analysis to focus on target market.
❖ Responsible for selecting, ordering, and promoting the sales of sportswear to achieve over $125,000 in sales over a six-month period.
❖ Demonstrated skills in leadership, organization, and group motivation.
❖ Supervised sales staff of fourteen.
❖ Sold custom-made sportswear.
❖ Examined and evaluated markets through on-site observations.

Employment History
Assistant Director, Public Relations
Morris Brothers, Sioux Falls, SD, 2003–present

Management/Marketing Assistant
S.D. Management Services, Inc., Sioux Falls, SD, 1999–2003

Promotion Coordinator/Sales Representative
Athletics West, Sioux Falls, SD, 1996–1999

Education
B.A., 1993, Business and Marketing, University of Vermont, Burlington

References available on request

Lucille Sirios

392 Alturn Drive • Geneva, IL 60134
Home (815) 555-8372 • Work (312) 555-3846 • lucillesirios@xxx.com

OBJECTIVE

Advertising staff of a major international publishing house. Particularly interested in a position that will utilize my written and verbal fluency in German.

PROFESSIONAL EXPERIENCE

Berlin American, Chicago, IL, Manager and Buyer, 2003–present
- Develop, produce and implement direct main and newspaper advertising campaigns that have directly contributed to a 45 percent sales growth over four years.
- Buy and merchandise German textile and ceramic handcrafted items.
- Maintain financial control of $375,000 annual sales volume.
- Translate business-related documents, German/English and English/German.

Books, Etc., Bookstore, Minneapolis, MN, Manager/Regional Planner, 1999–2003
- Responsible for effective visual presentation for three area stores.
- Trained and supervised ten employees.
- Controlled inventory and financial planning of $300,000 annual sales volume.

La France, Edina, MN, Counter Manager, 1995–1999
- Supervised staff of twelve waiters.
- Supervised food preparation and distribution.
- Integrated daily cash receipts into restaurant financial budget.

EDUCATION

St. John's University, Collegeville, MN
Bachelor of Arts in Government and German, June 1999

Institutes for American Universities, Berlin, Germany
German language coursework, 2003

References Available

DR. MARVIN A. ROBINSON

Office: (205) 555-3928 • 89 Fairview Place • Huntsville, Alabama 35804
Home: (205) 555-3346 • 44 Buck Drive • Huntsville, Alabama 35804
marvinrobinson@xxx.com

OBJECTIVE
A managerial position with state government in which I may put my experience
and skills in administration to best use.

EDUCATION
Ph.D., University of Iowa, School Administration, 1995
M.S., Louisiana State University, Baton Rouge, Secondary Education, 1986
B.S., Louisiana State University, Elementary Education, 1984

EMPLOYMENT
Superintendent, Huntsville Schools, Alabama, 2002–present
Superintendent, Park School District, Prattsville, Alabama, 2000–2002
Principal, Mission High School, Montgomery, Alabama, 1995–2000
Principal, Jackson Heights Public School, Jackson, Alabama, 1993–1995
Assistant Principal, Jackson High School, Jackson, Alabama, 1990–1993
Math Teacher, Hopewell High School, Mobile, Alabama, 1986–1990

SELECTED AFFILIATIONS
* Alabama Association of School Administrators
* American Association of School Administrators
* State Superintendent's Advisory Committee
* State Department Evaluation Committee
* Chamber of Commerce
* Jobs Plus, Board of Directors
* Leadership Development Program, Huntsville School District and University of
  Alabama
* Louisiana State University, Graduate Instructor
* University of Alabama, Graduate Instructor

SPEAKING ENGAGEMENTS AND CONSULTING PROJECTS

* Baton Rouge, Louisiana, National Association of Secondary School Principals, "A Climate for Learning"
* Toronto, Ontario, National Association of Secondary School Principals, "The School Administrator Under Stress"
* National Academy for School Executives, Keynote Speaker, "Educational Accountability: Three Approaches"

PUBLICATIONS

* "The Road to Being a Superintendent," *NASSP Bulletin 34*, no. 2
* "Looking to the Future in American Education," ERIC
* "Educational Approaches in African American Schools," Alabama Department of Education, e-newsletter, November 1998

HONORS

* Talladega College, Member, Board of Trustees
* Huntsville Chamber of Commerce, Outstanding Educator Award, 1997
* Louisiana State University, President, African American Student Union
* *Who's Who in American Colleges and Universities*

References available on request

LANE TYLER
1892 Red River Road
Toledo, Ohio 43601
(419) 555-2078
lanetyler@xxx.com

Objective	A position as Instructor of Business and Marketing
Education	
2003	M.B.A, Ohio University, Athens
1995	B.A., State University of New York at Buffalo
Experience	
2003–present	Director of Marketing, Business Unit Leader, Foodservice, Pillar Paper Company, Toledo, Ohio
Responsibilities:	Strategic and marketing leadership with profit and loss accountability for a $310 million commercial foodservice business. Develop a competitively advantaged business by providing distinctive marketing, products, and services that support customer and operator needs. Direct development of environmental strategies for paper products. Provide manufacturing with objectives and standards for raw material, sourcing, quality improvement, and cost reduction. Lead business planning process.
Accomplishments:	Increased division earnings by 17 percent in 1994. Initiated a new products development program. Introduced operator-focused marketing programs to pull product through distribution.
2001–2003	Senior Marketing Manager, Commercial Products Division, Pillar Paper Company, Toledo, Ohio
Responsibilities:	Led development and marketing of new high performance products and systems for towels and soaps. Developed and led a foodservice venture for the Commercial Products Division. Managed integration efforts with the Foodservice Corporation. With sales management, developed target market strategies.

Accomplishments: Led development and marketing of a new towel brand which contributed over $1 million in new earnings within eighteen months. The foodservice venture generated $2 million incremental earnings in 1993. Awarded one of three Business Excellence awards for my contributions in 2002–2003.

1999–2001   Senior Marketing Manager, Foodservice Division, Pillar Paper Company, Toledo, Ohio

Responsibilities: Directed marketing and development for 650 foodservice products. Developed foodservice strategies that aligned with commercial towel and tissue business objectives. Directed Marketing Communications programs.

Accomplishments: Improved Specialty Products earnings by 10 percent in 1999 and 2000 with a balance of marketing programs and price guideline development.

1996–1999   Director of Marketing and Sales, American Convenience, Inc., Toledo, Ohio

Responsibilities: Reported to the president and directed all sales and marketing functions, with accountability for continuous earnings and improvement. Responsible for product and program development, advertising, customer service, and a twenty-five person sales staff.

Accomplishments: Initiated a national accounts program. Introduced American's first sales incentive program which helped drive a 12 percent increase in sales and profits in the first year.

References Provided on Request

Anders Washington

3554 Front Street #306
Gallup, New Mexico 87321
(505) 555-2283
anderswashington@xxx.com

Career Ambition
Teaching and research position with a major medical center or hospital.

Related Experience
Good Samaritan Hospital, Gallup, New Mexico
Emergency Room Registered Nurse, January 2000 to present
- Trained new emergency room nurses and technicians with appropriate ER procedures
- Triaged all incoming patients and worked with EMT staff to stabilize patients
- Assisted physicians with suturing and casting
- Administered IVs and medications
- Provided emergency medical care, including CPR
- Supervised nursing staff of emergency room during night and weekend shifts

Central Albuquerque Community Hospital, Albuquerque, New Mexico
ICU/CCU Registered Nurse, January 1997 to November 1999
- Supervised nursing staff on weekends
- Coordinated nursing and lay teams in providing emotional and psychological support for terminal patients and their families
- Monitored temporary pacemakers; assisted with insertion of intra-aortic balloon pumps; interpreted 12-lead electrocardiograms; inserted catheters and IVs; assisted doctors with examinations and administered required medications; assisted with cardioversions
- Instructed outpatients recovering from open-heart surgery and myocardial infarction

Related Experience (continued)

Buck Ambulance, Albuquerque, New Mexico
Emergency Medical Technician, September 1992 to January 1995

- Responded to emergency calls for medical assistance
- Triaged patients on site and prepared for transportation to hospital or medical center facilities
- Assisted hospital medical personnel in transfer of patients and emergency room care
- Administered IVs and various types of emergency medical intervention

Education

R.N., University of Santa Fe, New Mexico, 1997
EMT, University of Santa Fe, New Mexico, 1991

Memberships

- Sigma Theta Tau, Nursing National Honor Society
- American Association of Critical Care Nurses
- National Hospice Nurses Association
- American Heart Association, volunteer instructor
- American Red Cross, volunteer instructor

References available on request

Muhhamed Al-Fulani

2114 Renton Street • Kirkland, WA 98005 • (206) 555-3497
M.Al-Fulani@xxx.com

CAREER OBJECTIVE

Engineering position with industrial manufacturing company.

CAPABILITIES

- Manage continuous fire furnaces that produce flat pressed glass and glass for machine and hand blowing.
- Plan and supervise all aspects of furnace operation and maintenance, including personnel scheduling and staffing.
- Evaluate alternative production methods and materials to reduce costs and improve product quality.
- Control raw materials inventory, ordering, and inspection.
- Train employees in use and maintenance of equipment, including computer-assisted operations.
- Review product availability and equipment developments to keep systems up-to-date for both production and safety concerns.
- Plan, coordinate, and supervise all aspects of glassware production.

ACHIEVEMENTS

- Initiated improved method for raw materials handling that resulted in $250,000 in actual savings.
- Worked with production engineers to develop new heating procedures that made furnaces 20 percent more efficient in start-up time.
- Developed operating procedures that improved worker safety.
- Designed alternative casting method using AUTOCAD that reduced external temperatures dramatically, thus decreasing fire and burn hazard.
- Given Award of Merit for developing material composition that produced greater clarity in present glass products.

WORK HISTORY

1995–present	Pihuck GlassWorks Factory, Kirkland, Washington Furnace/Production Manager
1984–1995	Boeing, Renton, Washington Senior Technician, Instrumentation Casing Section

EDUCATION

2003	B.S., Engineering, University of Washington
1993	A.A., Technology and Industry Production, Everett Community College, Everett, Washington

References available on request.

ADRIAN KASIMOR

389 North Bend
Iowa City, Iowa 52240
(319) 555-2243
adriankasimor@xxx.com

OBJECTIVE:

A position involved in the management of a conference center or conference services

EXPERIENCE:

Assistant Director, Iowa Summer Quarter, 2000–present, University of Iowa, Iowa City
• Direct administrative operations, University of Iowa Summer Quarter.
• Make policy decisions and direct long-range planning.
• Responsible for program development and communications with vice-presidents, academic deans, department chairs, and academic unit personnel.
• Manage the development, preparation, and justification of budgets and accounting operations.
• Direct marketing and publicity campaign.

Conference Administrator, 1995–2000, University of Iowa, Iowa City
• Managed biannual international seminars.
• Produced brochures, made registration and site arrangements, and developed and maintained operating budget.
• Coordinated additional conferences, seminars, and workshops.

Administrative Assistant, 1992–1995, University of Iowa, Iowa City
• Managed/supervised Academic Records Department.
• Assisted in start-up operations of University Conference and Performing Arts Center.

EDUCATION:

University of Iowa, Iowa City
B.A., Psychology, 1991

Other Courses and Workshops:
• Supervision
• WordPerfect Desktop Publishing
• The New Supervisor/Manager
• Practical Ways to Improve Your Communication

References available on request

◆ DAVID SAMUELS ◆

84 Bayonett Street
Chattanooga, TN 34701
(615) 555-9388
davidsamuels@xxx.com

◆ SUMMARY

Sales and marketing manager who wishes to enter the publishing industry as a sales representative or sales manager. Proven leadership ability to conceptualize, structure, and achieve both market and profit objectives.

◆ PROFESSIONAL EXPERIENCE

National Sales Manager, 2004–present
Washington Paper, Subsidiary of PaperGraphics, Inc., Chattanooga, TN

▼ Assumed total responsibility for sales of commodity and specialty papers in the United States and Canada with total sales in excess of $50 million.

▼ Coordinated with manufacturing the transfer of specialty paper manufacturing to another mill.

▼ Upgraded mill from commodity to specialty paper producer.

▼ Created and implemented the Neighborhood Business Strategy, concentrating sales efforts to develop business close to the mill, effectively reducing costs and improving profit sales incentive program to motivate the sales force to generate new product sales.

▼ Initiated aggressive sales efforts for additional volume, allowing increased production, using idle equipment, which spread costs and substantially improved profits.

Sales Manager, 1995–2004
Repro-paper, Inc., Subsidiary of PaperGraphics, Inc., Buffalo, NY

▼ Managed sales of all copy-type papers, representing 40 percent of sales.

▼ Directed department of six sales professionals.

▼ Reduced dependence on major accounts by expanding customer base and raising prices.

▼ Improved profitability stressing quality, service, and elimination of volume price contracts, which were depressing profits.

▼ Changed company image perception from volume supplier to top-quality product producer dedicated to customer service.

▼ Supported our customers through National Trade and Industry Association participation.

◆ PROFESSIONAL EXPERIENCE (continued)

Product Manager, 1992–1995

Specialty Papers, Greenfield Paper Company, Subsidiary of PaperGraphics, Inc., Greenfield, MA

▼ Assumed newly created position, established its function, and made it work profitably.

▼ Established specifications and pricing and developed marketing strategies.

▼ Consolidated product lines in greeting card, wallpaper, photographic, and flameproof markets.

▼ Developed trade names, product identification, and customer recognition.

▼ Implemented advertising campaigns with assistance from ad agencies.

▼ Worked with technical department to develop technical bulletins and supporting materials in the greeting card, wallpaper, photographic, and flameproof markets.

▼ Worked closely with regional salesmen and their customers to develop greater product use and customer satisfaction.

◆ EDUCATION

B.S., Business, University of Pittsburgh, Pennsylvania

◆ AFFILIATIONS

▼ American Marketing Association

▼ Chattanooga Business Alliance

▼ Chattanooga Chamber of Commerce

◆ HONORS

▼ Excellence in Marketing Award, AMA, 1995

▼ Mayor's Certificate of Service, 2002

▼ Businessperson of the Year, 2003

References available on request

FAITH NGUYEN

775 SW Tillbury Road • Fresno, CA 93723
(203) 555-7623 • faithnguyen@xxx.com

CAREER OBJECTIVE:
Project Management Director

EXPERIENCE:
Communications Manager, Consortium of California Counties, Fresno, CA, 2003–present

The Consortium administers an annual federal grant of $25 million for employment and training programs in 35 counties. As the first Communications Manager of the Administrative Office, I developed and implemented a public relations effort for the Job Training Partnership Act (JTPA).

Highlights:
- Develop annual report, e-newsletter, brochures, and other materials to market program's job training services to private business, public sector, and job seekers.
- Received National Business Alliance Distinguished Performance Award.
- Conceived and managed a statewide conference for employment and training professionals; hosted visiting International Fellowship representatives from four European countries.
- Directed work of advertising agency and support staff.
- Coordinated communications among various branches and county officers.
- Designed and maintained systems for recruiting, selecting, and training members of the Private Industry Association of California and local elected officials of the CCC Board of Directors.
- Managed quarterly meetings and biannual retreat.
- Supervised effort to diversify funding resources for the CCC.
- Coordinated multimedia job seeker recruitment campaign used in 26 states.
- Responsible for tracking state and federal legislation with potential impact on CCC programs.
- Prepared testimony and information for legislators.
- Attended state legislative hearings.

EXPERIENCE: (continued)
Risk Manager, Consortium of California Counties, Fresno, CA, 2001–2003

Developed and implemented risk management system to assure limitation of program risks and compliance with federal and state laws. Served as liaison to district branch offices and state, regional, and federal offices of the Department of Labor in the interpretation and implementation of laws and regulations.

Highlights:
- Developed system of procedures to identify and monitor program risks.
- Conducted comprehensive Risk Management Reviews of district for compliance with state and federal laws.
- Responsible for development, training, and implementation of EEO/AA policy and Affirmative Action Plan. Investigated and processed complaints.
- Developed grievance procedure and trained all CCC managers statewide.

Personnel Director, International Paper Suppliers, San Francisco, CA, 1992–2001

Responsible for Industrial Relations functions and monitoring of EEO/AA activities for corporation with 95 corporate locations nationwide. First woman in the corporation's history to hold this position. (Hired in Corporate Communications Department in 1988.)

Highlights:
- Interpreted and administered labor contract and represented the company in local and master bargaining.
- Developed corporate policy manual on EEO/AA. Designed a brochure for corporate use and conducted regional EEO/AA seminars in corporate supervisory training courses.
- Coordinated corporate community programs.
- Worked with field managers to prepare for government regulations compliance review.

EDUCATION:
B.A. in Communications, Stanford University, CA, 1988

Portfolio and references available upon request

Joseph W. Caldwell

346 Buena Vista • Pocatello, ID 83251
(208) 555-6682
josephcaldwell@xxx.com

Job Goal

Construction foreman for housing construction company.

Skills

- Experienced in a wide range of construction and wood products occupations.
- Thorough knowledge of indigenous woods and their suitability for construction.
- Twenty years of supervisory experience.

Work History

Supervisor, Twin Peaks Plywood, Pocatello, ID
Trained and supervised mill workers in all areas of mill operation. Scheduled shifts of 24 workers each, three shifts a day. Worked relief schedule on weekends. Developed safety awareness program. Monitored safety procedures. Consulted with SAIF inspectors for methods of improving working environment safety. Employed continuously from 1998 to present.

Shift Foreman, Idaho Lumber Supply, Boise, ID
Supervised splitters, pullers, and saw operators on day shift. Trained workers in all aspects of lumber mill operation. Monitored safety procedures. Employed initially as mill worker; worked seasonally from 1992 to 1998 (moved).

Carpentry Crewman, Dales Construction, Boise, ID
Worked on carpentry crew building residential dwellings and office complexes in Boise and environs. Experienced with foundation work, roofing, sheetrocking, and finish carpentry. Worked seasonally from 1989 to 1998 (moved).

Work History (continued)

Woodworker, Ames Oak Furniture, Boise, ID
Operated lathe, power saw, miter saw, drill press, scroll saw, burnishing sander, and other power equipment in the manufacture and finishing of oak furniture. Employed full-time from 1987 to 1989 (business relocated out of state).

Education

Boise Central High School

Memberships

International Mill Workers Local #655
Carpenters Local #2815

References available on request.

Janet Lee Kosh
2314 Sunnyview Drive NW
Springfield, MO 65812
(417) 555-9076
janetleekosh@xxx.com

Professional Objective:

Seeking new challenges in a position as communications director in a private-sector corporate environment.

Previous Experience:

Director of Communications, City of Springfield
Springfield, MO, October 2001 to present
• Plan and direct public information program for the City of Springfield.
• Supervise city management communications with the general public and corporate representatives.
• Coordinate writing, design, and production of city's annual report to taxpayers, newsletter to local businesses and the chamber of commerce members, and brochures covering important aspects of city planning.
• Consult with business leaders, civic leaders, and public arts organizations on fundraising programs for community-wide projects.

Director of Communications, Office of Development,
Washington University
St. Louis, MO, 1993 to 2000
• Planned communications strategies and programs for corporate, individual, and alumni fundraising efforts.
• Directed public information program: wrote and distributed press releases and feature articles, coordinated and secured necessary design services, planned and developed new public information and publication projects as needs were identified.
• Responded to information requests from the general public, university faculty and students, and alumni.
• Coordinated interdepartmental fundraising tracking system and communications.

Page 1 of 2

Publications Coordinator, Cartwright/Haeuser/Martinez Architects
St. Louis, MO, 1988 to 1993
• Wrote, edited, and submitted articles to professional and trade journals;
  prepared entries for architectural awards programs.
• Maintained project books and photo and slide files for use in client
  presentations.
• Developed presentation graphics; contracted with designers.
• Produced general office graphic materials, including 240-page bound
  promotional book.

Honors & Awards:

Gold Award, Two-Color Publications, CASE National, 1993
Silver Award, One-Color Publications, CASE National, 1992
Gold Award, Capital Campaign, CASE National, 1992

Education:

Bachelor of Arts, Graphic Design/Writing (dual major)
Washington University

Continuing Education Conferences & Workshops:

Design and Communications for Corporate Publications
Dallas, TX, 2003

City Manager's Association Conference
Annually, 2001–present

Getting Things Done, Career Track Seminar
Vancouver, BC, Canada, 2001

Desktop Publishing Seminar, *Publish* Magazine
San Francisco, CA, 2000

CASE Conference on Capital Campaign Communications
Indianapolis, IN, 2000

References and portfolio furnished upon request.

Norton W. Walters

10563 SE Powell Blvd.
Tulsa, Oklahoma 75135
(918) 555-4436
nortonwalters@xxx.com

Personal Focus

Financial analysis and strategic marketing management

Professional Experience

Financial
Financial analysis, cash flow analysis, securities analysis, business and economic forecasting and feasibility studies.

Marketing
Market analysis and testing, strategic planning and administration, market research, opinion polling and analysis, coordinating and facilitating focus groups.

Management
Program and project management, staff supervision, budget preparation and administration, MIS reviews and management audits, public relations, staff development, personnel recruitment and selection, union contract interpretation and administration, Affirmative Action and EEO compliance planning and administration.

Communication
Team building, employee relations counseling, dispute resolution and mediation, public speaking, report writing, group facilitation.

Employment History

President and CEO, Step One Enterprises, 2004–present
Began and manage trading and brokerage corporation with affiliations in China, Hong Kong, Taiwan, and the Philippines. Sold business after achieving personal and professional goals.

Employment History *(continued)*

Consultant, Various corporate and public sector clients, 2001–2004
Provided business consulting services in market analysis, marketing strategy and planning, public relations, budgeting and financial analysis.

Division Manager, State of Oklahoma, Human Services, 1990–2000
Managed job development and placement with staff of 24. Conducted program evaluation and planning. Developed public relations program and hired personnel. Served as liaison to Governor's office for employment issues.

Education

Master of Business Administration, Finance and Management
University of California, Berkeley, 2000

Bachelor of Arts, Philosophy
University of Colorado, Boulder, 1986

References furnished upon request

JANE P. HARPER
8395 Beaumont Drive
Lincoln, Nebraska 68508
janeharper@xxx.com

OBJECTIVE

A managerial position in a major Midwest private corporation that will maximize my proven abilities in:
• Administrative Management
• Organizational Development
• Corporate Affairs
• Public and Community Relations

SKILLS/EXPERIENCE

• Recruited, trained, and developed management teams of up to 15, supervising up to 2,800 employees.
• Successfully prepared and administered operating and capital budgets totaling up to $133 million.
• Experienced in initiating and overseeing all operating functions associated with capital improvement projects totaling $150 million.
• Developed marketing and public relations programs that generated significant private-sector business. Created public and private-sector partnerships that fostered substantial commercial and entrepreneurial growth.
• Guided operations analyses resulting in significant efficiency improvements and cost savings through changes in work processes and operating procedures, upgrades to management methods and systems, and reallocation and downsizing of workforce.

CAREER HISTORY

Chief Executive Officer, City of Lincoln, Nebraska
• Recruited in 1996 to improve the financial situation, strengthen organizational planning and development, as well as establish better communication and information management systems.

CAREER HISTORY *(continued)*

- Responsible for administrative and business affairs including management staffing, budgeting, finance, employee relations, service programs, and community relations.
- Initiated multilevel operations analysis used as basis for creating new strategic plan.
- Identified and led planning, design, and completion of capital improvement projects totaling more than $150 million.
- Supervised development of business plan that reduced operating costs $800,000 in key corporate component.
- Initiated analysis and guided development of internal organization to better manage labor relations and employee benefits functions. Eliminated two-year backlog of unresolved worker compensation cases.
- Led and implemented reorganization that resulted in creation of central data processing and management information services functions.

General Manager, City of Greeley, Colorado
- Recruited in 1994 to unify and upgrade administrative systems/procedures and gain better control of finances.
- Responsible for all day-to-day operations.
- Introduced coordinated management reporting system that yielded significant improvements in internal/external communications, management decision making, and organizational efficiency.
- Adapted existing budget to modified zero-base budgeting system.
- Reversed trend of economic base erosion by working with existing businesses to foster expansion and improve competitiveness.

Previous experience includes progressive general management positions in public sector organizations in Florida, Oklahoma, and Maine.

EDUCATION

Master's Degree, 2000
Marcus Graduate School, University of Ohio, Athens

Bachelor's Degree, 1995
Bates College, Lewiston, Maine

References provided on request

JOELLA BAKER

3932 North Vista
Tucson, AZ 85726
(602) 555-3828
joellabaker@xxx.com

OBJECTIVE

A position in public relations or promotion that will require my organizational, communications, and planning skills.

PROFESSIONAL EXPERIENCE

Office Manager, Health Consortium, Tucson, AZ
2005–present

Organize and direct all company office activities including interviewing, selecting, training, scheduling, and supervising office support personnel; oversee administration of employee benefits plans and assisting with claims. Assist in compliance to Arizona Safety Board reporting regulations.

Establish effective procedures and policies; oversee quality performance of customer service, public relations, and clerical activities; troubleshoot complex and/or sensitive customer problems. Plan work flow assignments to successfully meet all established deadlines and management objectives; interact effectively with all departments to provide highest levels of efficiency and to maintain excellent standards of customer service.

Assist controller with cash management and other financial duties including banking negotiations and procedures pertinent to Chapter 11 status.

Proficient in use of IBM and compatible ACCPAC accounting and word processing systems and software, including Microsoft Office and Lotus Notes.

Credit & Collection Manager, Health Consortium, Tucson, AZ
2001–2005

Responsible for reviewing and verifying company credit applications and setting credit limits for clients. Developed and recommended appropriate changes in credit policy to management. Processed authorized orders, prepared invoices, credited account payments, and tracked past due amounts. Sent late notices and negotiated customer payment arrangements for collection of delinquent account balances.

PROFESSIONAL EXPERIENCE (continued)

Customer Service Manager, Health Consortium, Tucson, AZ
1995–2001

> Made direct contact with customers and prospective clients; maintained highest possible customer service standards. Maintained current knowledge of sales and special promotional events; served as support and backup for marketing/sales force.

> Provided customers with general and technical product information and special assistance. Promptly resolved order and/or account problems; ensured that orders were received; interacted effectively with other company departments; tracked order shipments through contact with freight company representatives.

> Conducted customer research projects to determine amendments and/or new, improved features and service policies.

Receptionist/Cost Accounting, Penobscot Wire & Cable, Everett, MA
1993–1995

> Answered and directed incoming/outgoing switchboard calls; verified job cost information; performed daily calculations and maintained accurate and current bookkeeping records; responsible for miscellaneous clerical assignments.

EDUCATION AND TRAINING

B.A. in Business Administration, 2005
University of Arizona, Tucson, AZ

References available on request.

JEFFERSON BIRD

3829 High Road • Warwick, RI 02887
(401) 555-9287 • jeffersonbird@xxx.com

OBJECTIVE
A position in engineering in the public sector

BACKGROUND SUMMARY
Over twenty years experience in construction and mechanical engineering for private corporations, specifically: field engineer for installation of propulsion turbine plant on land-based test site; industrial and product engineering in the shipbuilding, material handling, chemical, and gas industries in construction, maintenance, engineering, and administrative capacities.

EDUCATION
M.S., Mechanical Engineering
Eastern University, Springfield, MA

B.S., Mechanical Engineering
Pennsylvania Institute of Technology, Pittsburgh, PA

EXPERIENCE
Senior Engineer, 2002–Present
Newport Shipbuilders, Inc., Warwick, RI
- Supported construction and operating personnel during installation, start-up, and testing of propulsion, generator, and hydraulic machinery.
- Performed facility survey, prepared technical reports, and provided engineering support during construction, set-up, and testing of the propulsion turbine plant.
- Assisted in construction during structural and mechanical equipment support and foundation.
- Coordinated fabrication and installation of full-size mock-up for integrated sub-base turbo generator.
- Provided support to designers, draftsmen, and construction personnel to ensure compliance with technical specifications and code requirements.

Page 1 of 2

EXPERIENCE (continued)
Engineering Supervisor, 1994–2002
Shipbuilders Corporation, Providence, RI
- Designed various mechanical and fluid systems and assisted in procurement, installation, and testing of systems and equipment.
- Designed and assisted in construction and testing of flow-through crude oil handling system on 120,000-ton double-hull tanker, reducing initial cost and increasing operational efficiency.
- Organized a multidisciplinary team to develop and build an oil-water separator to meet pollution control requirements.
- Conducted equipment and system test at the factory and after completion of installation for various components, including pumps, heat exchangers, hydraulics, and control/monitoring devices.
- Assisted in installation and testing of bulk petrochemical heating system to maintain the product temperature.

Staff Engineer, 1990–1994
TEC, Fiber Division, Boston, MA
- Assisted during installation, start-up, and testing of machinery for fiber, film, cellulose, and bulk material and processing equipment.
- Developed and assisted in installation of automated overhead conveying system to replace manual material handling operation for cellulose sheet.
- Supervised installation of the filling line to increase bagging output for microcrystalline cellulose.
- Redesigned the PVC blown film machine and provided assistance during installation and start-up.

Assistant Engineer, 1988–1990
Pennsylvania Oxygen Corp., Ltd., Pittsburgh, PA
- Supervised workforce of 120 with responsibility over production and maintenance for oxygen and acetylene plant and facilities.
- Conducted the economic analysis for relocating oxygen plant.
- Supervised erection of the plant at the new site.

References on Request

Deanna Smith

3476 W. Seventh • Las Vegas, NV 89133
(702) 555-4756 • deanna.smith@xxx.com

Career Goal

Director or Administrator position with government agency.

Achievements

* Directed administrative operations for college continuing education program.
* Made policy decision with regard to operations management and communications.
* Responsible for long-range planning and program development.
* Acted as liaison to department directors and college top administration.
* Managed development, preparation, and justification of accounting and budgeting operations.
* Coordinated annual international seminar, including registration, accommodations, travel and site arrangements, budgeting, and production of brochures.
* Supervised department of academic records.
* Coordinated conferences, seminars, and workshops with a variety of government and private organizations.
* Assisted in start-up operations of conference center.
* Experienced with corporate general ledger bookkeeping, auditing, payroll, and year-end closing.
* Experienced with credit management, credit reviews, and collections.

Employment Experience

Assistant Director, 2003–present
Continuing Education, University of Nevada, Las Vegas, NV

UNLV Conference Center
Conference Center Associate Administrator, 2000–2003
Management Assistant, Continuing Education, 1999–2000
Assistant to the Director, Continuing Education, 1994–1999
Administrative Assistant, Continuing Education, 1992–1994
Secretary, Continuing Education, 1990–1992

Corporate Accounting, 1988–1990
Miller & Sherwin, Engineering Associates, Las Vegas, NV

Accounts Receivable, 1984–1988
Caesar's Palace, Las Vegas, NV

Education

B.A. in Business Administration, UNLV, 2003

Las Vegas Business College, Office Management, 1990

References

Available as requested.

SUNIL RAJAH

1233 Mission Street • San Pablo, CA 98329
(212) 555-0812 • s.rajah@xxx.com

GOAL

Obtain a sales or marketing position requiring analysis and strategic planning

EDUCATION

Oregon State University, 2003
M.B.A., Marketing

Massachusetts Institute of Technology, 1989
M.S., Civil Engineering

University of California, Los Angeles, 1987
B.S., Engineering

EXPERIENCE

Civil Engineer, CH2M Hill, Inc., 2000–present
- Responsible for analysis and design of transportation systems.
- Coordinated planning and construction with city, state, and federal government.
- Successfully negotiated contract for $26.8 million in highway construction for the city of Los Angeles.
- Responsible for developing cost-benefit ratios, staff and material estimates and schedules, and project budgets.
- Experienced with computer-aided design, drafting, and structural analysis.

Engineering Sales Specialist, Shell Oil Company, 1990–2000
- Responsible for home heating oil sales program and technical support for distribution companies.
- Designed and implemented a marketing program for potential distributors that resulted in a 23 percent increase in sales over the previous year.
- Developed a network of technical support for both distributors and end users of the product.

HONORS

Who's Who in Engineering, 1999
Chapter President, Society of Women Engineers, 1999–2003

REFERENCES

Available on request

DAVID J. MASTERS

169 Broad Street * Concord, NH 03301 * (603) 555-3948

david-masters@xxx.com

CAREER OBJECTIVE
Marketing associate with the advertising department of a major retailer

EDUCATION
* Continuing Education coursework, Concordia College, 2002 to 2004
  Business courses in Marketing, Management, and Advertising
* Bachelor of Science, Library Science, Boston University, 1981

EMPLOYMENT RECORD
Research and Development Specialist, Public Relations Department, New Hampshire Job Training Program, Concord, NH, 1994 to present.
* Provide job market consulting services, prepare program proposals and contracts, coordinate activities with consultants, and handle customer service.
* Complete study of present and future needs of the administrative unit and district offices, including capability of service delivery based on anticipated funding.
* Draft and implement a plan for research and development activities, with primary emphasis on identifying funding sources.
* Develop and maintain videos, training programs, and individual resources. Supervise staff of seven; serve as liaison to county offices.

Research Librarian, Business and Technology Department, County Library, Concord, NH, 1986 to 1994.
* Maintained active records on resources for research in business and technology.
* Responded to queries from library patrons for research resources.
* Worked with individuals to develop research plans for using library resources.
* Remained current with new developments in the field.
* Supervised staff of five.

Associate Librarian, New Hampshire State Library, Concord, NH, 1981 to 1986.
* Maintained all state, local, and federal government publications.
* Developed catalog of publications available at the state library facility.
* Supervised library interns in cataloging project for state library system.

References available on request

ALICIA CARPENTIER

3890 West Arlington • Syracuse, NY 13201
(315) 555-3294 • aliciacarpentier@xxx.com

OBJECTIVE

A position as music department director at a public high school

OVERVIEW

Over ten years experience as a private instrumental, voice, and music theory teacher. Founder and director of Santos, a Renaissance choral and instrumental group. Coordinated fundraising for the Arts Council: established goals, formulated policies, and organized efforts.

EMPLOYMENT HISTORY

2005–current

Director of Fundraising, Syracuse Community Arts Council, Syracuse, NY
Develop fundraising programs. Coordinate solicitation and disbursement of funds. Establish fundraising goals and policies for collecting contributions. Establish relationships with local, regional, and national organizations and coordinate events, support bases, and contacts.

2000–2005

Assistant Publicist, Syracuse Community Arts Council, Syracuse, NY
Wrote press releases, delivered presentations, and designed fliers and posters announcing competitions and events. Organized community events. Coordinated the 1994 Arts in the Park celebration in downtown Syracuse.

1995–2005

Private Music Instructor, Syracuse, NY
Taught voice, piano, and violin lessons on an individual basis. Instructed children and adults in basic music theory and technique.

RELATED ACTIVITIES

2001–current
Founded performance group focused on Renaissance music. Coordinated extensive research on early instrumentation, authenticity of performance. Act as director, arrange scores, and organize performances for the nonprofit chorus Santos.

2000 and 2001
Conductor of Student Orchestra, New York State Music Festival

1995–2001
Member, Sacred Choir of Syracuse

1995–2001
Member, Oberlin Conservatory Chorus; Member, A Cappella Choir

EDUCATION

M.A. in Renaissance Music History and Instrumentation, 1997
State University of New York, Syracuse, NY

B.A. in Musical Performance and Direction, 1995
Oberlin Conservatory of Music, Oberlin, OH

References Provided Upon Request

EVELYN TICKEL

4987 Broadway
Boulder, CO 80304
(303) 555-3892
evelyntickel@xxx.com

Objective
A position as a high school science or environmental studies teacher

Education
University of Colorado, Boulder, CO
Teaching Certification, grades 1-12, 2005

Colorado State University, Fort Collins, CO
Bachelor of Science, Zoology, 1982

Professional Experience
Instructor, Boulder County Environmental Education Center,
Boulder, CO
Instructed classes in zoology, environmental ecology, and plant and tree identification, using classroom and outdoor hands-on techniques. Supervised overnight trips for high school-aged students. Developed and wrote booklet on endangered Colorado wildlife for use as a textbook. Volunteer, part-time staff, 2003–present.

Biological Assistant, University of Colorado Wildlife Department,
Boulder, CO
Participated in capture, tagging, and relocation of bighorn sheep in Colorado, and in dietary studies of large ungulates. Assisted in research of black-capped chickadees: made sonogram recordings, maintained 75 birds. Assisted in research of endangered fish species in Western Colorado rivers: collected fish, identified species, collected data, performed literature search, and compiled and condensed information. 2001–2003.

Professional Experience *(continued)*

Consultant, Pokahu Ranch, Maui, HI

Developed and wrote a conservation plan for the protection and restoration of the native ecosystem. Researched and evaluated the natural history, recovery plans, regulations, and recommendations of government officials. Performed species counts and determined the possibilities of rehabilitation of disturbed lands, eradication of pests, and reintroduction of endangered species. April–June 2003.

Scientific Technician, Washington State Department of Fisheries, Olympia, WA

Assisted in biological studies to assess the use of natural and artificial habitats by marine fish species for the purpose of developing criteria for habitat protection, mitigation, and enhancement. Collected and compiled data on salmons for habitat protection and harvest management protection purposes, including species identification, length, weight, scale sampling, sex, mark sampling, tagging, and red salmon spawning "nests" identification. Identified marine micro-invertebrates for fish stomach analysis. Performed herring and smelt spawn surveys, plankton tows, beach seines, and eelgrass samples. Interviewed sport and commercial fishers. Led Web research and compiled critical data in a searchable database. Prepared data summaries, charts, illustrations, and graphs. Various departments, 1982–1999.

References provided upon request

MARGARET HALVORSEN

154 Shoreline Drive • Chicago, IL 60611 • (312) 555-1707
margarethalvorsen@xxx.com

OBJECTIVE
Technical Writing and Editorial Management

HIGHLIGHTS OF QUALIFICATIONS
- Researched and wrote science biographies for technical reference books.
- Developed and wrote employee training manuals, catalogs and brochures, advertising copy, and press materials for retail businesses.
- Wrote and edited a broad range of grant proposals for technical and lay audiences.
- Developed, wrote, and designed public relations and fundraising materials.
- Strong background in word processing, desktop publishing, and graphics software on Macintosh and IBM computer platforms, including Photoshop, Acrobat, Illustrator, and more.

WORK EXPERIENCE
Director, Corporate & Foundation Relations
University of Chicago Office of Development, Chicago, IL,
2003–present

Grant Writer, Fundraising & Development Office
University of Chicago Press, Chicago, IL, 2000–2003

Promotions Manager and Events Coordinator
Pattersen's Books, Chicago, IL, 1990–1995

EDUCATION
Columbia University, B.A. with Distinction, Phi Beta Kappa, English with Creative Writing Emphasis, 1990.

Additional coursework included microbiology, chemistry, calculus, geology, statistics, and computer science.

WRITING PORTFOLIO AND REFERENCES AVAILABLE

ABDUL RAHMAN

345 Coral View, Apt. 9B * Coral Gables, FL * 33128
(305) 555-7823 * abdulrahman@xxx.com

OBJECTIVE

Production management position with a process-color printing firm

---

SUMMARY

* More than 25 years experience in all aspects of printing technology and production.
* Technical background in publishing, graphic arts, printing, and systems.
* 15 years in printing and department management.
* Developed innovative programs for cost-savings and increased productivity.
* Experienced mechanical engineer with thorough knowledge of printing equipment.

CAREER EXPERIENCE

MANAGER OF GRAPHIC ARTS ENGINEERING, 1998 to present
D.E.C. Printing Group, Southeastern Division, Miami, FL
* Specified and managed $175 million in lithography for 12 printers in the division.
* Enhanced profitability as a result of involvement in procurement, planning, printing, and quality assurance programs and the introduction of technological innovations.
* Directed 80 professional and technical people in 5 departments at the central plant.
* Worked closely with management in Quality Assurance/Target Management program, which increased efficiency by a margin of nearly 35 percent.

PRINTING OPERATIONS ENGINEER, 1990 to 1998
Graphic Color, Subsidiary of D.E.C. Printing Group, Miami, FL
* Operated and maintained working conditions for 7 Heidelberg 6-color presses.
* Designed work flow process that increased efficiency and press production by 20 percent.
* Supervised crew of 20 press operators and 5 technicians.
* Worked closely with stripping and camera departments to ensure highest quality press output.

EDUCATION

B.S., Mechanical Engineering, Arizona State University

References available on request

Pamela Miles

33 Hardesty Lane, Apt. 34 • Tallahassee, FL 32303 • (904) 555-9283
pamelamiles@xxx.com

Objective

An art teacher position at the primary or secondary school level.

Education

Teacher's Certification for primary and secondary art instruction, 2005.
B.S., Art (Humanities and Social Sciences), Florida State University.

Qualification Highlights

- Certified to teach art in Florida.
- Experienced with teaching grade school children arts and crafts projects at Children's Activity Center.
- Knowledgeable about art media and techniques, including digital imaging programs.
- Experienced at planning schedules, events, and programs.

Professional Work Experience

Director of Development Communications
1996–present, Office of Development, Florida State University,
Tallahassee, FL.
Plan and direct the public information program of the FSU Office of
Development. Organize the design and production of organizational
publications and plan the annual publications schedule. Gather information
and write news releases and feature articles.

Publications Coordinator
1993–1996, Searway/McKenna/Morris/Planners, Raleigh, NC.
Wrote, edited, and submitted articles to professional/trade journal.

Associate Editor, *The Biological Science Record*
1990–1994, American Association of Biological Scientists, Tallahassee, FL.
Designed *The Biological Science Record*, a quarterly publication of the
College of Biological Sciences.

Professional Work Experience *(continued)*

Designer, Display Advertising Department
1986–1990, *Florida Sun-Times*, Tallahassee, FL
Designed advertisements, prepared layouts, created artwork and
promotional ads, sold advertising; handled general administrative/record
keeping duties; organized and conducted tours of the plant.

Relevant Activities

- Member, Tallahassee Art Alliance, 1996–present.
- Volunteer, Children's Activity Center, 2001–present.
- Computer Graphic Art Workshop, Compaq Headquarters, Inc.,
  Tallahassee, FL (one day).
- Desktop Design and Publishing Seminar by Robert Parks, Tallahassee, FL
  (seven days).

References

Provided on request.

Angelina Bergman

884 NW 12th Avenue
Fort Worth, Texas 76109
(214) 555-1985 (daytime)
(817) 555-9712 (evening and weekend)
angelabergman@xxx.com

Summary of Qualifications

General management executive with 15 years experience in corporate sales, marketing, customer service, development, and distribution.

Experience

DaMark-Dolin America Corp., 2000–current
A $640 million Fortune 500 public corporation serving the cosmetics industry.

EXECUTIVE VICE PRESIDENT, Dallas, Texas, 2004–current
Catalog and Commercial Division. Direct sales, marketing, customer relations, and distribution for a two-plant, $180 million sales operation. Combined two acquired companies into the second-largest corporate division. Eliminated $325,000 in duplication costs. Designed national marketing strategy that produced a 15 percent sales increase. Generated 30 percent increase in new-business sales by expanding and upgrading product production. Increased profits by a margin of 23 percent in one year by enlarging client base and controlling prices. Improved quality control and productivity by reorganizing departments and centralizing support functions.

CORPORATE OFFICER AND VICE PRESIDENT, Houston, Texas, 2000–2004
Corporate Management Division. Directed strategic acquisition business development, marketing, and venture subsidiaries. Directed major capital expenditures, business plans, and incentive programs for twelve business units. Formulated corporate mission and established long-range strategic plan, which led to supervision of major restructuring decisions. Completed several acquisitions and strategic divestitures that expanded the corporate profit margin approximately 18 percent.

DIRECTOR OF CORPORATE DEVELOPMENT, Houston, Texas, 1993–2000
Corporate Management Division. Spearheaded four years of product design and diversification, resulting in the corporation's first major market breakthrough in the pharmaceutical industry. Managed all business and venture development, including acquisitions, new technologies, start-ups, joint ventures, and leasing agreements. Directed development of a new manufacturing line of medicinal lotions through acquisition of Soltero, Inc. Improved plant productivity by 15 percent.

Early Career Positions, 1985–1993

Operations Management, WemCo Inc., Houston, Texas
Design Module Leader, Patterson Corporation, Houston, Texas
Project Team Leader, Patterson Corporation, Shreveport, Louisiana

Education

Louisiana State University, M.S., Chemical Engineering & Business
University of Montana, B.S., Mechanical Engineering

References available on request.

KEVIN L. BAUER

3890 43rd Avenue • Ann Arbor, Michigan 48106
(313) 555-3892 • kevinbauer@xxx.com

CAREER SUMMARY

General management executive with significant broad-based experience in consumer, manufacturing, and publishing businesses. Technical background in publishing, graphic arts, printing, and systems.

Proven leadership skills and expertise in:

- Sales
- Strategic Planning
- Marketing
- Business Development & Acquisitions
- Operations Management
- Financial Analysis

PROFESSIONAL EXPERIENCE

D. D. WILLIAMS CORPORATION, 2001–Current
A $1 billion Fortune 500 public corporation serving niche printing and graphics/video markets.

Executive Vice President, Santo Catalog and Commercial Group
Ann Arbor, Michigan, 2003–Current

- Directed sales, marketing, customer services, estimating, and distribution for a two-plant, $125 million sales printing operation.
- Combined two acquired companies into the second largest corporate business group, eliminating $250,000 in duplication.
- Designed a national, market-driven strategy that delivered a 17 percent increase in sales.
- Generated new business sales of 30 percent in response to expanded and upgraded manufacturing equipment requirements.
- Increased profits 28 percent through focus on prospecting and pricing control. Improved control and productivity by reorganizing sales assignments and centralizing sales support functions.

Corporate Officer and Vice President
Oshkosh, Wisconsin, 2001–2003

- Key member of Corporate Management (executive) Committee with broad strategic, acquisition, business development, and marketing responsibility and authority in lean and highly autonomous corporate structure.
- Directed major capital expenditures, business plans, and incentives for 12 autonomous business units. Key board member for venture subsidiaries.
- Formulated corporate mission and market strategy, which led to major restructuring decisions.

Page 1 of 2

◆ Completed the purchase and transitionally directed the Peters Companies, adding five new subsidiaries and two new print markets and expanding sales by more than $200 million.

◆ Accomplished other acquisitions and strategic divestitures, including the sale of the Flexible Packaging Group (two plants, $50 million sales) and the decision to divest the video group (five companies, $45 million sales).

◆ Established the long-range strategy for the D. D. Williams Publications Groups (two plants, $43 million sales) and the strategic plan to create the D. D. Williams Pre-Press Group (three plants, $18 million sales), including the group management organization and start-up of Color Response–Minnesota.

◆ Spearheaded a corporate identity campaign that emphasized D. D. Williams's national scope; developed a new corporate name that sparked investor and Wall Street interest.

GREETING CARDS, Inc., 1990–2001
A $1.5 billion market leader in consumer and publishing products.

Director of Corporate Development
Kansas City, Missouri, 1999–2001

◆ Spearheaded four-year diversification program resulting in Greeting's first major acquisitions of Beel & Craig ($254 million sales) and SSN (educational, specialty, and consumer software publisher).

◆ Managed all business/venture development, including acquisitions, new technologies, start-ups, joint ventures, and licensing agreements.

◆ Directed an electronics venture and an acquired educational software subsidiary.

Manager of Graphic Arts Engineering
Kansas City, Missouri, 1995–1999

Operations Manager
Kansas City, Missouri, 1990–1995

EDUCATION
University of Massachusetts, Amherst
M.S., Industrial Engineering, 1989

University of Tennessee, Knoxville
B.S., Mechanical Engineering, 1987

References available on request

JONATHAN B. OWENS

2245 RIVER ROAD • NEWPORT, OR 97366

(503) 555-2435 • jonathanowens@xxx.com

OBJECTIVE

After twenty years of active duty in the Coast Guard, I am seeking a management position in Program Development and Implementation that will utilize my extensive background in these areas.

EXPERIENCE

2005–present: Branch Chief for Emergency Medical Central Training Center, U.S. Coast Guard, Newport, OR

Responsibilities

Developed, designed, and implemented the curriculum for training Coast Guard personnel. Responsible for selecting and evaluating staff of 30. Managed an annual budget of $200,000 for staff training and operations.

Contributions

Established new computer system to improve communications utilizing electronic mail. Developed and implemented new internal and external valuation programs to test new performance-based curricula. Designed and implemented new instructor development plans, which included continuing educational programs for personnel.

2003–2005: Operations Officer, U.S. Coast Guard, Ilwaco, WA

Responsibilities

Scheduled all ship movement activities. Supervised program for conducting boardings at sea to ensure compliance of commercial and recreational vessels to federal law. Supervised 20 personnel, including training and evaluation.

Contributions

Developed new unit training program by fostering a supportive educational environment.

2001–2003: Operations Officer, U.S. Coast Guard, Bethel, AK

Responsibilities

In charge of vessel traffic control for the safe passage of large crude oil carriers traveling in and out of Prince William Sound. Managed work schedules for both vessel traffic and communications watch standing personnel. Responsible for training, development, and performance evaluations for 15 personnel. Managed the maintenance of a remote microwave communications and vessel traffic radar system for all of Prince William Sound.

Contributions

Installed new radar tracking system that included upgrading remote power supply unit for one radar site. Improved personnel watch rotations to maximize time spent on the job as well as improve flexibility of time off. Implemented the hiring of civilian employees to replace Coast Guard personnel as permanent watch standers in the Vessel Traffic Center. Improved relations between Coast Guard and Maritime Industries.

1997–2001: Administration Officer, U.S. Coast Guard Marine Safety Office, Ilwaco, WA

Responsibilities

In charge of personnel and supply administration for a 50-person unit. Direct supervisor for seven personnel, including training and performance evaluations. Managed an annual budget of $350,000 for the maintenance and upkeep of an office building and a 29-unit housing complex.

Contributions

Centralized administrative personnel to take a team approach to handle all unit administrative matters. Eliminated unnecessary reports. Expedited the process of all administrative work by purchasing new computer hardware and software to increase efficiency.

1994–1997: Instructor, Leadership School, U.S. Coast Guard, San Diego, CA

Responsibilities

Involved with developing, designing, and implementing curriculum for newly established leadership and management program for Coast Guard personnel.

Contributions

Developed two-week curriculum for the school from the latest leadership and management practices. Participated in design, development, and testing of the new performance evaluation system currently used by the Coast Guard.

EDUCATION

Master of Arts in Educational Administration, University of Oregon, Eugene, OR

Bachelor of Science in Human Relations and Organizational Behavior, University of Oregon, Eugene, OR

REFERENCES AVAILABLE UPON REQUEST

MARCIA PENAS SMITH

55 Alexandria Street, Apt. 25 • Washington, DC 20013
(202) 555-0988 • marciapenassmith@xxx.com

OBJECTIVE

A position as translator for a federal or state agency

LANGUAGES

Fluent in written and spoken English, Spanish, Portuguese, and French

EDUCATION

M.A. in Spanish and Portuguese, 1998, Middlebury College, Middlebury, VT
B.A. in French and Psychology, 1988, Arizona Sate University, Tempe, AZ
Foreign Study Program in Oaxaca, Mexico, 1985–1986

WORK EXPERIENCE

English Teacher, English Department, Madrid University, Spain, 1994–1999
*Taught reading and conversation to undergraduates and teachers of non-English
majors. Developed curriculum for and taught elective reading course on North
American short stories. Taught beginning conversation to small group of primary
school students. Informally advised Spanish students on living and studying in
the U.S.*

Assistant to Director, Office of International Education, Arizona State System
of Higher Education, Arizona State University, 1986–1994
*Developed and administered Latin American summer exchange program for high
school students. Assisted with foreign student and foreign study orientation programs.
Coordinated visits of international guests. Assisted in administration of foreign study
programs.*

Office Assistant, Office of International Programs and Summer Session,
Arizona State University, 1978–1986
*Assisted in administration of overseas programs. Assisted with information meetings
and predeparture orientations. Gave general advising to students interested in study
and work abroad. Handled summer session and special programs registrations.
Responsible for general secretarial-receptionist duties.*

REFERENCES AVAILABLE

ANNA ROBINSON

P.O. Box 389
Cheyenne, WY 82001
(307) 555-2983
annarobinson@xx.com

OBJECTIVE

To teach at the secondary school level

EDUCATION

- M.Ed. and Certification, University of Colorado, Greeley, 2005
- B.A., Elementary Education, University of Michigan, Ann Arbor, 1987
- Wyoming Real Estate Broker's License, Rocky Mountain School of Real Estate, Cheyenne, WY, 1998
- Wyoming Real Estate Sales License, Professional Institute of Real Estate, Laramie, WY, 1994

RELEVANT EXPERIENCE

- Reading and Writing Tutor and Student Teacher, Greeley School District, Greeley, CO, 2004–2005
- Advisor, Entrepreneurial Youth, Inc., Cheyenne, WY, 1999–present
- Classroom Teacher, grades 1 through 7, specialization in Language Arts, Tyler School District, Tyler, MI, 1987–1994

PROFESSIONAL EXPERIENCE

Designated Broker, Sales and Marketing Director, Courtmore Homes, Inc., Cheyenne, WY, 1998–2003
Responsibilities included development of purchase contract package; contract approval; design of brochures, advertising, model home complexes; consultation concerning land acquisition and development; hiring, supervision, and support of subdivision sales staff and decorating personnel.

Sales Representative, Homeland, Inc., Cheyenne, WY, 1994–1998
Responsibilities included subdivision sales, contract writing, buyer relations and closings, and sales office/model complex management.

REFERENCES AVAILABLE ON REQUEST

PETER J. LUCERO

3876 Maple Street • Topeka, KS 66603 • (913) 555-9835
peterlucero@xxx.com

CAREER OBJECTIVE

A career position in international relations or operations with a multinational corporation or major organization.

SUMMARY OF SKILLS

- Multilingual administrator, educator, lecturer in Spanish, German, French, and English.
- Associate pastor and director of a Chicago inner-city parish complex, an upwardly mobile Catholic community in Kansas, and a popular parish in Frankfurt, Germany.
- Regional consultant to the New York electronic media.
- Member, Board of Directors, for a nonprofit housing development corporation.
- Director of professional, paraprofessional, and volunteer staffs in four countries.
- Coordinator of private- and government-sponsored relief activities for Central American refugees.
- Chaplain and advisor to international business and diplomatic communities.
- Liaison between church authorities, civic officials, and professional groups in the greater Frankfurt metropolitan area.
- Academic advisor to graduate students on University of Kansas campus.

CAREER HISTORY

Assistant Administrator, Associate Pastor, St. Mary's Church
Topeka, KS, 2003–2004
- As member of religious education staff, recruited, trained, and evaluated performance of 100 volunteer teaching/clerical support personnel.
- Created and conducted adult seminar groups, stressing contemporary moral and ethical problems.

Assistant Administrator, Catholic Archdiocese
Frankfurt, Germany, 2000–2003
- Initiated German-American lecture series on sociopolitical, moral, and religious themes.
- Regularly presided at multilingual liturgical functions in international congregations.

CAREER HISTORY
(continued)

- Provided pastoral counseling in three languages to French, English, and German speaking communities in Frankfurt.
- Liaison between church officials and civic, business, and diplomatic leaders.
- Supervised educational programs for parish residents and their children.

Member, Administrative & Counseling Staff, Graduate Student, Jesuit College of Theology
Boston, MA, 1996–2000
- Served as academic advisor and pastoral counselor to resident graduate students while pursuing doctoral degree.
- Assisted in developing efficient administrative structures, challenging curricula, relevant practice, and appropriate criteria for the selection and training of those destined for ministry.

Assistant Administrator, Missionary Project
Tegucigalpa, Honduras, 1995–1996
- Served all levels of local, national, and international society in Honduras, from campesinos and refugees to professional and business classes and diplomatic personnel.
- Assisted in the pastoral and material care of these groups, focusing on the plight of displaced persons, the educational and health-care needs of indigenous populations, and the training and development of their civic, political, and religious leaders.
- Acted as liaison between these groups and international relief agencies.

Chaplain of St. Rose's Home
Chicago, IL, 1993–1995
- Served as chaplain at this home for terminally ill cancer patients.
- Attended to the spiritual, psychological, and counseling needs of patients and their families.
- Recruited, trained, and monitored performance of more than 100 volunteers.
- Performed traditional functions of active clergy in major urban hospital environment.

EDUCATION
- Catholic Institute of Germany, Frankfurt, Germany, S.T.D./Ph.D. Candidate
- Jesuit College of Theology, Boston, MA, S.T.L. (advanced Master of Arts), Magna Cum Laude
- Harvard Divinity School, Cambridge, MA, M.Div.
- St. Peter College, Newport, RI, B.A. Cum Laude, Sociology/Philosophy

REFERENCES AVAILABLE

• JoAnna Weber

P.O. Box 34
Phoenix, Arizona 85034
(602) 555-0938
joannaweber@xxx.com

• Objective:

Office manager for travel agency, with opportunity to train in tour management.

• Experience:

Office Manager, Saxton Microflox
Phoenix, Arizona, 2003–Present
Responsible for all central support operations, bookkeeping staff, and office planning and administration. Maintain payroll records, process federal and state tax reports. Handle cost accounting and general ledger reports. Direct hiring and supervision of office staff. Respond to requests from engineering and executive departments for special project support.

Travel Coordinator, Saxton Microflox
Phoenix, Arizona, 2001–2003
Responsible for coordinating all travel arrangements for engineers and executives traveling nationally and internationally. Processed payments and payment vouchers. Maintained data file of travel resources.

Secretary, West Phoenix School District
Phoenix, Arizona, 1995–2001
Provided secretarial support to principal and faculty. Extensive public relations contact with students, parents, faculty, and general public. Responsible for bookkeeping and supply inventory. Supervised central office staff.

• Education:

A.A. degree, Office Systems, Salt Lake Business College
Salt Lake City, Utah

References on Request

Juanita Rodriguez-Sutton

330 Hollywood Boulevard • Los Angeles, CA 90063
(213) 555-2475 days • (213) 555-0248 evenings • j-rodriguez-sutton@xxx.com

Career Objective
Seeking position as Advertising Director for a large West Coast agency.

Achievements
- Handled distribution, retail marketing, advertising, and mail order marketing for weekly news magazine with more than two million circulation.
- Wrote advertising copy and made sales presentations to clients and account executives.
- Handled advertising accounts worth in excess of $1.5 million as Marketing Promotions Director for FM radio station.
- Developed thorough knowledge of domestic and overseas regulations for trademarks.
- Assisted marketing director with radio and television promotion and retail marketing.
- Coordinated radio and print interview opportunities for visiting artists and writers.
- Developed and implemented print and broadcast advertising campaign for major retail chain.
- Directed research department for market data and sales reports.

Work History
LA Productions Weekly, Los Angeles, CA
- Marketing Director, 9/04 to present
- Public Relations Director, 6/02 to 7/04

KBOQ Radio, Venice, CA
- Marketing and Promotions Director, 5/97 to 6/02
- Promotions Assistant, 3/97 to 5/97

Macy's, San Francisco, CA
- Marketing Department, 6/92 to 3/97

Education
University of California, Los Angeles
- Postbaccalaureate study in Advertising and Marketing, 9/00 to 6/02
- B.S. in Journalism/Public Relations, 6/92

References available on request.

Joseph Monroe

3892 Beverly Road • Springfield, MA 01101
(413) 555-3982 • josephmonroe@xxx.com

Objective:

A position in marketing and sales management at a radio station that would utilize my skills as a corporate executive and my extensive experience in sales management in the manufacturing field.

Education:

M.B.A., University of Massachusetts, Amherst, 2000
B.A., Business Administration, Communications and Radio, Ohio University, Athens, 1984

Professional Experience:

Vice President of Sales & Marketing, Amco Corporation, 2000–present
• Develop marketing strategies to support customer and operator needs.
• Coordinate between administrative, sales, and operations branches to provide manufacturing with standards and goals.
• Oversee relations with 50 top customers, representing more than $250 million in annual revenue.
• Supervise 20 sales staff and coordinate with Operations and Administration departments.
• Negotiated product and service charges with U.S. Postal Service, maintaining cost standard for a savings of $1 million over 5 years.
• Improved productivity by 45 percent in two-year period with design and implementation of employee participatory program.
• Supervised a marketing and promotion effort that saw sales improve 15 percent in the first quarter after implementation.

Sales and Marketing Manager, Amco Corporation, 1985–1999
• Supervised all salespeople.
• Negotiated contracts with 20 top customers.
• Managed all customer fulfillment and complaints.
• Responsible for development and marketing of product changes and new services.

Professional Experience: *(continued)*
- Negotiated new and renewed contracts with 20 customers, representing an annual revenue of $100 million.
- Established a standard sales training program in-house, which improved efficiency and consistency in customer relations.

Station Manager, WIML Radio, Ohio University, 1983–1985
- Managed budgets and staffing schedules.
- Supervised fundraising and programming, scheduling and publicity for radio station.

Programming Director, WIML Radio, Ohio University, 1982–1983
- Planned, reviewed, and revised all programming for station.
- Scheduled all on-air personnel.
- Hosted a classical and interview program.

Memberships:
- Board member, Corporation for Public Radio, Massachusetts
- Supporting member, Springfield Symphony
- Member, Marketing Association of America

Professional and personal references furnished on request.

JEAN K. SCHUMANN
389 SW 13th AVENUE • OLYMPIA, WA 97301 • (206) 555-3982
jeanschumann@xxx.com

CAREER OBJECTIVE
To obtain a position as Scientific Technician for the Washington Department of Fisheries or the U.S. Department of National Resources.

SUMMARY OF EXPERIENCE
• Collected biological data as Biological Aide at Washington Coastal Aquarium.
• Participated in field study emphasizing terrestrial vegetation, geological features, and marine organisms, and maintained field journal of activities, including plot studies.
• Compiled environmental report for county sub-area plan, producing vegetation map, writing and editing sections of report, and presenting group results to planning committee.
• Maintained records of shipments, collected and prepared ore samples for chemical analysis, and assisted in surveying for Taber Shipments, Inc.
• Developed and implemented Marine Biology (Intertidal Organisms and Rocky and Cobbled Shore Habitat) and Cedar and Salmon Natural and Cultural History Programs for use at Girl Scout camps.
• Assisted in supervising and training staff, planning programs, and evaluating performance and programs.
• Taught and led nature activities for children and adults in marine and terrestrial biology, intertidal habitats and organisms, forest ecosystems and habitats, botany, zoology, and meteorology.

WORK HISTORY
Community Resources Staff, Campus Recreation Center, Deschutes University
Olympia, WA, 2003–present

Assistant Director, Program Planner, Rainier Girl Scout Council
Tacoma, WA, 2000–2003

Program Development Intern, Rainier Girl Scout Council
Tacoma, WA, 1999

Biological Aide, Washington Coast Aquarium
Long Beach, WA, summers 1995–1999

Biological Assistant, Taber Shipments, Inc.
Spokane, WA, 1994

EDUCATION
B.A. in Biology, Deschutes University, Olympia, WA, 1999

References available on request.

GAVIN MCCLOUD

P.O. Box 12, St. Paul, MN 53402
(612) 555-0932
gavinmcloud@xxx.com

OBJECTIVE
A position as a high school science teacher

EDUCATION
University of Minnesota, Twin Cities, Minneapolis, MN, 2004,
Master of Education
University of Vermont, Burlington, VT, 1982, Bachelor of Science

PROFESSIONAL CERTIFICATION
Minnesota
Elementary 1–6
Middle and High School, 7–12

RELATED SKILLS AND EXPERIENCE

- Taught classes in stream ecology, outdoor survival, backpacking, and trip planning. Supervised overnight trips for primary and secondary school students. Assisted in programs and designing courses aimed at integrating science education with outdoor activities.
- Assisted in research on stream ecology and effects of pollutants: collected samples and other data, performed literature searches, and compiled and condensed information.
- Prepared data summaries, chart illustrations, and graphs; wrote summary reports; evaluated methods, procedures, and results of stream ecology studies.
- Assisted in biological studies to assess natural and artificial habitats by woodland species for developing habitat protection, mitigation, and enhancement criteria.

EMPLOYMENT HISTORY
Instructor, Minnesota Outdoor Center, St. Paul, MN
Part-time staff, 2004–present

Biological Assistant, State of Minnesota Wildlife Department,
Minneapolis, MN
1982–2004

References provided upon request

J. WILLIAM CLARK
4437 WHITE OAKS DRIVE • URBANA, Illinois 61801
309-555-2847 (VOICE) • 309-555-3345 (FAX) • jwilliamclark@xxx.com

OBJECTIVE
An executive position in an organization involved with public policy and finance.

PROFESSIONAL EXPERIENCE
Lecturer, Management and Public Administration
Graduate Center, University of Illinois, Urbana-Champaign, 1999 to present
Teach organizational management courses for the College of Business. Topics include Managing Organizations (process of organizing, planning, and controlling), Organizational Behavior (leadership, internal politics, and group dynamics), The Global Business Environment (domestic and international political, economic, and social issues that affect complex organizations), and Public Policy Administration (development, structure, and implementation of public policy).

Executive Consultant, Social Policy and Study Center
George Washington University, Washington, D.C., 1993 to 1999
Developed and taught seminars on organizational management and global economic issues for officials from the governments of fourteen countries. Coordinated the development of an Equal Employment Opportunity Plan for a major public policy research organization. Represented senior management with the government auditing agency requiring the affirmative action plan. Other principal clients included the Economic Policy Research Institute, the American Center for the Study of Behavior, and W. W. Group International, an organization that monitors and analyzes public policy issues throughout the world.

Assistant Executive Director, National School Boards Association
Washington, D.C., and Chicago, Illinois, 1988 to 1993
Planned, organized, developed, and coordinated programs and activities for the national network of school district trustees from the nation's urban centers. Consulted with the Director of the President's Commission on School Finance, the Executive Director of the Education Commission of the States, and the National Advisory Committee on Career Education.

PROFESSIONAL EXPERIENCE (continued)

Program Associate, National Public Schools Support Association
Washington, D.C., 1985 to 1988

Held full financial accountability for budgeting, planning, controlling, and personnel management. Provided consulting services to school districts and support organizations nationally.

Previous employment includes three years as a public school teacher in Illinois and four years active duty as an officer in the U.S. Navy.

EDUCATION

Ph.D. Politics and Public Policy Administration
George Washington University, 1992

M.B.A. Finance and Administration
Purdue University, 1985

B.A. Business and Economics (NROTC)
Purdue University, 1980

MEMBERSHIPS

National Field Task Force for the Improvement and Reform of American Education
U.S. Office of Education

Retired Naval Reserve Officers Association

REFERENCES ON REQUEST

KARL LI

290 Summit Drive
Portland, Oregon 97208
(503) 555-0709
karlli@xxx.com

OBJECTIVE:

A management position in sales or promotion for a quality manufacturing corporation.

PROFESSIONAL EXPERIENCE:

Executive Director (April 1996–present), Willamette Valley Health Care Foundation, Portland, Oregon

Provide direction for the Foundation. Responsibilities include strategic planning, fundraising, program development, volunteer development, and grant writing. Produce, sponsor, and coordinate the annual festival, Healthfest. Conduct a needs assessment for Willamette Valley as a measure of program effectiveness. Plan annual community fundraising campaign and membership campaign. Implemented the foundation's first online fundraiser, netting over $45,000 in its first year and doubling that amount the following year. Serve as Vice President of Oregon Non-Profits Association. On Portland Regional Hospital Finance Committee, Willamette Community Health Council, Oregon.

Regional Director (1991–April 1996), The Children's Foundation, Chicago, Illinois

Provided strategic management and hands-on assistance to 11 chapters in 9 states. Offered expertise in fundraising, finance, volunteer development, staff training, and programs. With chapter directors, established goals and objective for chapter performance. Evaluated achievements against goals. Hired, trained, and supervised chapter directors and regional offices staff. Directed 115 employees. Planned and conducted two training meetings per year for chapter directors and other key staff/volunteers. Acted as a resource to other regional directors on the subject of budgets, finance, and quantitative analysis. Served on the board of The National Children's Foundation, 1993–1996. Established a volunteer, region-wide database consisting of executive committee members and key volunteer leadership in 1993, with annual updates.

PROFESSIONAL EXPERIENCE: *(continued)*

Executive Director (1989–1991), The Children's Foundation, Midwest Region, Des Moines, Iowa

Responsible for the administration of the local chapter, including fundraising and program development. The door-to-door campaign led the nation in per capita revenue, the highest per capita to date, anywhere in the nation. Our largest sponsor-based event, Lifewalk, was expanded to the point where every community of 5,0001 held the event. Improved collection procedures and enhanced revenue. Influenced a reversal of Des Moines School Board policy to allow The Children's Foundation access to schools for fundraising.

Special Events Consultant (1988–1989), Des Moines, Iowa

Created two major fundraising events: bike treks and backpacking treks. Developed volunteer and corporate resources for special event fundraising in an agency heavily dependent on mail income.

Karl Li Advertising and Public Relations (1987–1988), Des Moines, Iowa

Provided advertising and public relations services to a variety of clients, both profit and nonprofit. Specialized in radio production/advertising.

EDUCATION:

Master of Public Administration (MPA)
University of Chicago, 1987

Bachelor of Arts, Communications (BA)
University of Chicago, 1985

REFERENCES AVAILABLE ON REQUEST

LUCINDA ALVAREZ

1283 Bramble Drive
Austin, TX 78710
(512) 555-1701 home • (512) 555-3602 office • lucindaalvarez@xxx.com

---

OBJECTIVE

To obtain a position as senior technical editor for a large corporation

---

EDUCATION

Columbia University, M.A., English. GPA, 3.91. 2003.
Columbia University, B.A. with Distinction, Phi Beta Kappa, English with
Creative Writing Emphasis. 1990.
Additional coursework included chemistry, calculus, geology, statistics, and
computer science.

EXPERIENCE

2003–present
**Proposal Writer, Corporate & Foundation Relations, University of Texas
Office of Development, Austin, TX**
Assist administrators and faculty in writing and editing a broad range of grant
proposals for technical and lay audiences. Develop, write, and design public
relations and fundraising materials for the university's maximum priority
projects. Review annual reports and other corporate publications to identify
major donor prospects. Conduct quarterly seminars for staff and faculty on
proposal writing. Supervise student assistant. During first year was involved in
generating gifts to the university totaling more than $3.1 million.

2002–present
Board of Directors, Fundraising Chair, Wild Rose Press, Austin, TX
Hold volunteer administrative and fundraising responsibilities for small
nonprofit literary press. Write and edit grant proposals to government agencies
and private foundations.

2000–present
Freelance Writer, Graphic Designer, and Photographer, Austin, TX
Services include color and black-and-white photography, desktop publishing,
and writing and editing newsletters, catalogs, advertisements, feature articles,
and public relations materials. Recent project involved researching and writing
science biographies for technical reference book.

EXPERIENCE (continued)

1990–2000
Promotions Assistant, University Book Stores, Inc., Austin, TX
Responsible for writing, designing, and producing store brochures, flyers, signs, and advertisements. Required extensive knowledge of desktop publishing, graphics, and production methods.

1985–1989
Program Manager and Events Coordinator, Drake's Books, New York, NY
Responsible for public relations and all aspects of weekly reading series at NYC's third largest independent bookseller. Designed and wrote all advertising copy, press releases, catalogs, brochures, and employee training manuals. Scheduled author appearances and hosted and introduced authors at events with audiences ranging from 50 to 400. Authors included Pulitzer Prize winners Taylor Branch and Tracy Kidder and National Book Award winner Stephen Jay Gould. Supervised a staff of two.

REFERENCES
Current references and writing samples available on request.

TAMARA MESERVEY

389 Southwest Fifteenth Avenue • Philadelphia, PA 19104 • (215) 555-2899
tamarameservey@xxx.com

GOAL

A production management position in advertising on a large circulation newspaper.

QUALIFICATIONS

- Experienced in all aspects of printing and prepress processing equipment, including digital imaging and desktop publishing software.
- Marketing, advertising, sales, and graphic production.
- Records management, including accounts payable/receivable, payroll, inventory control, and tax reporting.
- Purchase of supplies to assure adequate inventories.
- Day-to-day management responsibilities, including scheduling, assigning activities, training, and program assessments.
- Experienced with computerized typesetting and prepress graphic production.
- Public relations skills, including reception, sales, collections, and purchasing.
- Time management proficiency, promoting timely completion of projects and meeting deadlines.

EDUCATION

Community College of Philadelphia, PA, 2003–present
Business management courses with emphasis in retailing, advertising, marketing, accounting, and human relations.

Philadelphia College of Art, PA, 1992–1994
Associate of Arts Degree, Process and Camera Stripping.

EXPERIENCE

Management Assistant, Regional School of Ballet, Philadelphia, PA, 2002–2005
DUTIES: Learned and implemented managerial skills in daily management of dance school. Arranged advertising through local media sources. Planned development and marketing and advertising strategies. Completed billing reports, payroll records, compiled accounts payable and receivable information. Collected unpaid balances. Ordered and maintained inventories. Supervised staff and scheduled work hours.

EXPERIENCE (Cont'd)   *Camera Operator/Printer, Sir Speedy Printing, Philadelphia, PA, 1998–2002*
DUTIES: Operated variety of camera and bindery equipment, including printer and platemaker. Assisted customers, completed sales transactions and reports, prepared advertising for local media and yellow pages. Began system of tracking advertising results to better determine advertising cost-effectiveness.

Printer, In and Out Printing, Philadelphia, PA, 1994–1998
DUTIES: Operated printing machine and darkroom equipment. Coordinated incoming work assignments. Performed paste-up, platemaking, and bindery duties. Trained newly assigned employees. Composed, printed, and generated monthly newsletter.

REFERENCES AVAILABLE

THERESA MILLER

33528 Santa Monica Boulevard
Los Angeles, California 90088
(213) 555-8842
theresamiller@xxx.com

CAREER OBJECTIVE

Traffic manager for an advertising agency or corporate advertising department.

WORK EXPERIENCE

Connections Magazine, Hollywood, California
Production Manager, 2004–present
Oversee all aspects of production and printing for a national publication.
Involved in extensive client and advertising agency contact. Organize all art,
mechanicals, and final films. Coordinate with editorial and advertising
department heads for positioning of advertising. Work with graphic designers
on production specifications and proofing. Handle in-depth contact with other
media and service vendors. Produce copy and mechanicals for advertisements.

L.A. Arts Weekly, Los Angeles, California
Advertising Manager, 2000–2004
Directed advertising sales for 45-page arts section of *L.A. Times*. Developed sales
strategies, assigned territories to sales staff, conducted weekly sales report
meetings, tracked sales and billing. Coordinated advertising design and
production with graphic design staff. Directed preparation of mock-up ads for
sales presentations to encourage regular, increased ad sales for target clients.
Developed special ad pages for arts organizations and directed sales efforts.

Havener's, Burbank, California
Assistant to Promotions Director, 1994–2000
Conducted all in-store promotions and coordinated special events for large
department store. Placed advertising and publicity notices in local media. Wrote
text for radio and television spot announcements. Consulted on grand opening
of Hollywood store. Provided customer assistance.

EDUCATION

University of California, Los Angeles
B.S. in Advertising and Marketing, 1994

EDUCATION *(continued)*

Honors:
Cum Laude, 1994
Dean's List, 1992–1994
Wilma Morrison Scholarship, 1991–1994
National Association of Student Yearbooks, Advertising Sales Award, 1994
Best Advertising Design, 1994

MEMBERSHIPS

American Advertising Association
Women in Advertising
American Marketing Association
Magazine Publishers Inc.

References provided on request

ALETHA BESSEY

4893 ARLINGTON AVENUE
INDIANAPOLIS, IN 46201
(317) 555-9889
alethabessey@xxx.com

OBJECTIVE

A position in marketing with a strongly customer-oriented multinational corporation.

PROFESSIONAL EXPERIENCE

Research Scientist, International Feminine Care, Beverly Jones Corporation, Indianapolis, IN, 2003–present

> Evaluate, recommend, and develop product changes to meet performance expectation of a new feminine care product for three international regions of this Fortune 500 multinational consumer products company manufacturing such brand products as Bouncies and Comforts.

> Establish quantitative measures for subjective functional performance evaluations and product comparisons.

> Work closely with international marketing research department in suggesting and implementing improvements to consumer market research questionnaires.

> Design product development plans for market research efforts.

> Obtain medical clearances, coordinate materials, prepare product samples, and schedule equipment and testing.

> Work with U.S. product development group to integrate United States and international program support.

> Provide engineering with product information for equipment designs.

> Participate in regional project update meetings in the United States, Asia, Latin America, and Europe.

> Provide support to process trials in Mexico and Taiwan.

> Prepare reports on product functional tests.

> Participate on Product Development Seminar Committee to define format for company-wide seminar.

Scientist II, Scientist I, Senior Research Technician, Beverly Jones Corporation, Indianapolis, IN, 1997–2003

> Accountable for all aspects of product development for industrial wipers and washroom towels.

> Successfully developed new washroom hand towel product that out-performed market leader and returned twice the initial sales projections.

PROFESSIONAL EXPERIENCE *(continued)*

❯ Developed new market research techniques to define consumer language in describing products; translated and interpreted terminology for quantitative measures.

❯ Developed and validated mathematical model for determining user preference from physical test data.

❯ Developed several line extension products and implemented cost-saving technologies for existing products.

❯ Member of multifunctional business team; assisted in defining market needs, designing products to meet cost requirements, verifying advertising claims, providing technical sales support, and implementing product rollouts.

❯ Managed project budgets and established project objectives.

❯ Analyzed and resolved customer complaints regarding product performance; conducted one-on-one customer interviews and site visits.

❯ Provided process and product support for start-up of a new converting mill.

❯ Advised manufacturing personnel in conversion operations to ensure product quality and specifications; assisted in troubleshooting efforts.

❯ Wrote product specifications for manufacturing guidelines and worked with Quality Assurance for test methods and quality procedures.

❯ Consulted with packaging specialists to define packaging specifications.

Quality Assurance Superintendent, Techmill, Inc., Youngstown, OH, 1991–1997

❯ Organized and managed fifteen-person quality department for a new non-woven cloth manufacturing plant.

❯ Implemented corporate quality programs.

❯ Trained personnel and implemented statistical process control systems throughout the plant.

❯ Wrote and implemented a GMP manual for Class III medical device.

EDUCATION

M.B.A., Kennesaw State College
Kennesaw, GA, 1991

B.S., Mathematics/Engineering, University of Minnesota
Crookston, MN, 1989

REFERENCES AVAILABLE UPON REQUEST

STUART DAVID MARKS
66-B West 45th Street • Wilmington, Delaware 19835
(302) 555-8223 • stuartmarks@xxx.com

PROFESSIONAL OBJECTIVE
To bring my extensive experience as a certified accountant into the administration of a large metropolitan art museum.

EDUCATION
University of Chicago, M.B.A., 2003
Emphasis: Finance/Accounting

Illinois State University, B.S., 1998
Emphasis: Accounting

WORK EXPERIENCE
Corporate Accounting Manager, Bowles and Sharp, C.P.A.
1987 to present
• Direct staff of 27 certified public accountants and 15 support staff.
• Responsible for all corporate accounts, valued at more than $7.5 billion.
• Serve as liaison between accounting department and corporate CEOs.
• Reduced losses through implementation of cost accounting controls for two major corporate clients.
• Supervise corporate audits and hold final responsibility for federal and state reporting.
• Develop and maintain strategic corporate plans and accounting division budgets.

Certified Public Accountant, Truant Michaels & Associates, Inc.
1983 to 1987
• Handled ongoing accounting and reporting for 27 corporate clients.
• Prepared corporate and individual federal income tax reports.
• Audited corporate and public organization finances.
• Prepared financial statements for credit reporting and bank financing.

MEMBERSHIPS
Certified Public Accountants of Delaware
National Association of Certified Public Accountants

REFERENCES
Available upon request.

ANNA SEVIGNY

389 King Court
Springfield, MA 01101
(413) 555-2938
anna.sevigny@xxx.com

OBJECTIVE

An associate-level position in a public relations firm.

EXPERIENCE

Production Director, Cable Newscenter 7
Cable News Network, Springfield, MA, 2000–present
Supervise the development and airing of a one-hour cable news
show. Edit video footage. Handle all video while on air. Develop
and maintain strong communication with director, creating
consistency in the show's format. Provide support in maintaining
the flow of material.

Operations Engineer, WHHH-TV
Massachusetts Broadcasting Company, Springfield, MA, 1995–2000
Provided technical support and assistance for morning and mid-
morning news and commercial breaks, both local and network.

Public Relations Assistant, TIC AM/FM Cable
Springfield College, Springfield, MA, 1994–1995
Supervised the public image presented by radio station. Organized
a Charity Bowl-a-Thon that raised $2,000 for the Children's Care
Center of Springfield. Produced and co-wrote an audio
documentary about radio for local high school students. Developed
and distributed press releases for all station activities. Acted as
mediator during internal conflict.

EDUCATION

Bachelor of Arts, Speech Communication
University of Massachusetts, Amherst, 1994

Hannah Tober Scholarship for student showing greatest potential in
the field of Communications Management, 1994

REFERENCES AVAILABLE ON REQUEST

TOMIKA BROWN

3890 Park Avenue • Chicago, IL 60607
(312) 555-2998 • tomika.brown@xxx.com

OBJECTIVE

A position in a federal or state agency involving administration and project management

---

SKILLS HIGHLIGHTS

Management:

Program and project management, staff supervision, budget preparation and administration, public relations, staff development, human resources recruitment and selection, union contract interpretation and administration, Affirmative Action and EEO compliance planning and administration.

Communication:

Team building, employee relations counseling, dispute resolution and mediation, public speaking, report writing, group facilitation.

Financial:

Financial analysis, cash flow analysis, securities analysis, business and economic forecasting, project feasibility analysis, market analysis.

Computer:

Prime Mainframe, IBM, Macintosh, Lotus 1-2-3, Excel, Statview, 1-2-3 Forecast, WordPerfect, and MS Word.

PROFESSIONAL EXPERIENCE

Consultant, Hoffman & Monroe, Inc., Chicago, IL, 2000–present
Provide consulting services that include market analysis, marketing planning, strategic planning, public relations, and budgeting. Projects: Market research and business planning; human resources consulting regarding EEO and Affirmative Action guidelines, hiring strategies and practices; statistical analysis; and project planning and administration.

Partner, Sawyer, Collins & Co., Inc., Chicago, IL, 1990–2000
Principal in firm providing marketing analysis and planning, business forecasting and planning, and financial analysis for private firms and corporations.

EDUCATION

B.A., Business Administration and Management
University of Chicago, 1990

References available on request

Daniela A. Jamas

71 SW 15th Street
Sacramento, CA 95814
(916) 555-7321
danielajamas@xxx.com

Objective

A staff management position in a human resources firm or in a corporate human resources department.

Related Experience and Skills

- Developed and provided one-day seminars and a ten-week adult education class in social services advocacy through Pacific Community College.
- Experienced with group participation, lecture, and one-on-one instructional techniques.
- Supervised a staff of ten to develop community-wide needs assessment; set training goals and objectives; developed an audience-appropriate curriculum; coordinated speaker schedule; evaluated training results.
- Tutored middle-school students with special needs on a one-on-one basis.
- Coordinated social services to help individuals meet their needs for support, counseling, resources, and information in other support services.
- Worked closely with government, private social service agencies, and businesses to integrate services that best met individual needs.
- Implemented, produced, and edited various newsletters; wrote articles for several magazines.
- Familiar with IBM computers, well versed in Macintosh word processing and database programs.
- Semi-fluent with both written and spoken Spanish.

Work History

- Office Manager, Environmental Consultants, Inc., Sacramento, CA, 2005–present
- Marketing Director, All Seasons Windows, Sacramento, CA, 2001–2005
- Telemarketing Director, Raymond Bros., Inc., San Jose, CA, 1999–2001
- Manager, The Book Cover, San Jose, CA, 1996–1999
- Manager, Information and Referral Department of Public Affairs, Sacramento, CA, 1992–1996
- Teacher's Aide, Highland View Middle School, San Jose, CA, 1991–1992

Education

San Jose State University, B.S., 1991
Recreation and Leisure Studies, with minor in English

References available upon request.

ANNA JUAREZ
3892 Barbary Road
Sacramento, California 95813
(916) 555-9283
anna.juarez@xxx.com

OBJECTIVE	Buyer/Manager for an independent bookstore
EDUCATION	1990 M.L.S. University of Washington, Seattle 1985 B.A. Comparative Literature, University of California, Berkeley
PROFESSIONAL EXPERIENCE	2000–present Director, Media Services West Sacramento School District Direct the library services of 20 elementary, middle, and high schools in district. Supervise ten professionals. Designed the high school library media center of 50,000 print and non-print items. 1995–1999 Head Librarian Berryman School Library, Sacramento, California Directed the acquisitions and functioning of this school library serving 1,200 students and 95 professionals. Supervised five paraprofessionals. 1990–1995 Acquisitions Librarian Timberland Regional Library, Olympia, Washington Served as acquisitions librarian for this regional branch of libraries. 1985–1990 Teacher, Literature and Writing St. Mary's Girls Academy, Olympia, Washington Taught literature and writing courses to high school students at this private high school.

REFERENCES AVAILABLE ON REQUEST

ROBERT L. WILSON JR.

1854 S. Franklin Ave. • Chicago, IL 60647
(312) 555-8376 • robertwilson@xxx.com

OBJECTIVE

A position with a literary arts center or arts advocacy agency.

EXPERIENCE

Editor and Designer, 10/04–Present
Week's Worth Magazine, Chicago, IL
Started weekly arts, culture, and entertainment magazine, gaining a circulation base of 14,000 within four months. Manage all aspects of marketing and promotion. Supervise advertising department staff for ad sales and self-promotion advertising campaigns. Manage all aspects of production. Assign staff articles and edit freelance articles for publication. Design magazine from cover to cover. Manage budget and payroll for 15-person staff.

Editor, 4/02–9/04
Friday's Magazine, Illinois Daily News, Normal, IL
Assigned and edited staff stories. Created page layout and design. Wrote feature-length stories. Managed budget and 8-person staff for weekly entertainment magazine supplement to college newspaper.

Feature Writer and Columnist, 8/99–4/02
College of Arts & Sciences, Illinois State University, Normal, IL
Covered various entertainment events, wrote feature stories and weekly commentary column for Features department.

Staff Writer, 1/94–8/99
Communications Department, Illinois State University, Normal, IL
Community Relations Department. Assisted in the writing, design, and layout of a 12- to 24-page alumni newsletter.

EDUCATION

B.A. Communications (Fine Arts Minor), Illinois State University, Normal, IL, 1994

HONORS

- *Critical Film Review Award, Second Place, Illinois College Press Association*
- *Graphic Illustration Award, Second Place, Illinois College Press Association*
- *Public Relations Society of America*

References available on request.

ALFRED D. LANDERS

728 Bolero Court
Novato, CA 94945
(415) 555-2943
alfredlanders@xxx.com

OBJECTIVE

To play an integral role on a pastoral care team in a hospital or mental
health facility.

EDUCATION

Training Center for Spiritual Directors,
Taos Benedictine Abbey, NM, 2004.
• Intensive initiation into the art of spiritual direction.

Healing Ministries, Institute of Ministries,
San Jose, CA, 2001–2003.
• Formation and Advanced training, four semesters.

Clinical Pastoral Education, Mental Health, Coast Hospital,
San Jose, CA, 2000–2001.
• Internship, four units.

PASTORAL EXPERIENCE

2001–2004
Community Member, Taos Benedictine Abbey
• Participated in counseling and prayer ministry with members;
  participated in liturgies, retreats, and business office activities.
• Will complete training with an additional month-long program next
  year.

2000–2001
Chaplain Intern, Western Coast Hospital
• Pastoral focus on mentally ill legal offenders.
• Provided Eucharist ministry to patients in medical, surgical,
  neurological, geriatric, and adult psychiatric units.
• Participated in liturgy and prayer services.
• Provided pastoral interviews and counseling, including many religious
  denominations and nondenominational.

Page 1 of 2

JOB HISTORY

1994–present
Senior Commercial Lines Underwriter, Umbrella Insurance,
Group Department, San Rafael, CA

• Handle Oil Jobbers program in commercial group department, a
  nationwide program with heavy casualty, property, and inland marine
  coverage.
• Responsible for six states totaling in excess of $6 million annual
  premiums.
• Implemented company changes in underwriting practices and
  procedures.
• Developed 10-step program for profit. Audited current files.

1990–1994
Personal Lines Underwriting Supervisor, Umbrella Insurance,
San Rafael, CA

1985–1990
Property and Casualty Underwriter, Umbrella Insurance, Newark, NJ

References upon request.

MARIA NELSON

226 Highline #299 • Albuquerque, NM 87102
(505) 555-3872 • marianelson@xxx.com

OBJECTIVE

A management position in television or radio advertising in which my marketing and management experience can make a strong contribution to the organization as a whole.

WORK EXPERIENCE

Seven-Eleven, Albuquerque, NM
Regional Marketing Director, 2003–present
Developed a successful marketing campaign for a convenience store chain. Implemented marketing strategies to increase sales by 23 percent at the least profitable outlets. Initiated and maintained a positive working relationship with radio and print media representatives. Designed a training program for store managers and staff.

Arizona Register, Phoenix, AZ
Advertising Sales, 2000–2003
Sold space advertising to a variety of business and organizational clients. Maintained excellent communications with top clients. Made cold calls on businesses to encourage advertising. Responsible for 25 percent increase in regular advertiser base over four-year period. Coordinated with design and production departments to maintain quality in advertising products as client advocate.

Arizona Evening Herald, Phoenix, AZ
Classified Advertising Sales, 1996–2000
Sold classified advertising to private and business clients. Entered advertisements in computer system. Checked advertisements for accuracy. Billed clients for advertising. Made follow-up calls to increase run of advertising. Coordinated with advertising department on special issue discount offers in the classified section.

Other work experience includes advertising sales manager for student radio station, University of Arizona; sales clerk for women's clothing boutique; and door-to-door sales representative for children's books.

EDUCATION

University of Arizona, Phoenix, AZ
Bachelor of Science in Business, 1996
Advertising and Marketing Major, Communications Minor

Honors:
• Project Award for advertising campaign developed for student radio station
• Dean's Honor Roll
• Sigma Delta Gamma, advertising honorary

SEMINARS

Marketing Strategies in Advertising
American Marketing Association, 2004

Cooperative Advertising: Opportunities and Strategies
Arizona Press Association, 2003

References available on request.

Da'uud Hussein

389 Spring Rock Road • Missoula, MT 59806 • (406) 555-2009
d.hussein@xxx.com

Objective

A position in Human Resources Management for a manufacturing
corporation.

Qualifications

- Design systems for recruiting, selecting, and training clerical,
  production, and middle management personnel.
- Maintain and direct recruitment, selection, and training of those
  personnel.
- Develop, monitor, and implement EEO/AA policy and Affirmative
  Action Plan.
- Investigate and process complaints relating to EEO/AA.
- Develop corporate policy manual of EEO/AA.
- Conduct EEO/AA seminars and presentations.

Work History

Publicity Manager, Rocky Mountain Products
Missoula, MT, 2003–Present.
Hired as first Communications Manager of this wood products company
to develop and implement a public relations effort.

Assistant Personnel Manager, Rocky Mountain Products
Missoula, MT, 1998–2003.
Assisted in recruitment, selection, and training of clerical, production,
and management personnel.

Assistant Manager, Corporate EEO Programs, U.S. West Communications
Richmond, VA, 1990–1998.
Shared responsibility with corporate EEO/AA Officer for monitoring
equal employment opportunity and affirmative action activities for 95
corporate locations nationwide.

Education

B.A. in Communications, awarded 1987
Mary Baldwin College, VA

References available on request.

AMELIA NELSON

1545 Arboretum Drive, Apt. 34
Rutland, Vermont 05701
(802) 555-3828
amelianelson@xxx.com

OBJECTIVE

A corporate position in sales that involves extensive customer contact.

WORK EXPERIENCE

Public Relations Assistant

Applebury Inc., Burlington, Vermont, 2005–present.
Direct interface with clients and the public, assessing needs and providing solutions. Assist in product inquiries and setting up discounting programs for qualified customers. Represent company in trade shows. Exhibit strong product knowledge in handling customer complaints through analysis and evaluation of complaint report. Support for sales force and on-site technicians.

Management/Marketing Assistant

Divan Management, Rutland, Vermont, 1995–2005.
Assisted marketing research projects and conducted a general management survey for mini-warehouse industry. Coordinated promotional campaigns, utilizing database analysis to focus on target market.

Special Promotion Assistant, Sideline Sales

University Bookstore, Burlington, Vermont, 1992–1995.
Responsible for selecting, ordering, and promoting the sales of sportswear to organizations and a student body of 40,000 students, averaging more than $75,000 in sales. Demonstrated skill in leadership, organization, and group motivation.

Entrepreneur

Nelson Promotions, Burlington, Vermont, 1990–1992.
Sold custom-made sportswear to Greek system and dormitories. Examined and evaluated on- and off-campus markets through on-site observations and informal interviews. Supervised two employees.

EDUCATION

B.A., 1990, Business and Marketing
University of Vermont, Burlington

REFERENCES AVAILABLE ON REQUEST

PETER L. LARSON

3890 PEACH ROAD • ATLANTA, GEORGIA 30304
(404) 555-9888
peterlarson@xxx.com

OBJECTIVE

A position in the manufacturing industry that will utilize my extensive background in sales and sales management.

SUMMARY OF QUALIFICATIONS

➤ Results-oriented sales professional recognized for ability to develop and maintain productive long-term relationships with clients.
➤ Excellent track record of establishing new sales territories and attracting new clients.
➤ Expert in developing effective long-range marketing plans.
➤ Strong training and motivational skills, as demonstrated by the success achieved in developing successful sales teams.
➤ Outstanding public speaker with the proven ability to conduct effective and persuasive seminars and presentations.
➤ Successful at projecting accurate sales and budget forecasts.

EXPERIENCE

Assistant Director/Ground School Manager, 2000–present
U.S. Flyers, Chatham County Airport, Georgia
➤ Developed student enrollment for career flight academy.
➤ Utilize direct mail, telemarketing, and direct sales approaches to cultivate and qualify prospective students.
➤ Develop relationships with beneficial markets.
➤ Present promotional talks and seminars at job fairs, college campuses, and civic organizations.
➤ Act as liaison between students and school administrators.
➤ Monitor students' programs to ensure completion within designated time and budget parameters.

Sales Director, 1997–2000
Workshops, Inc., Atlanta, Georgia
➤ Developed direct mail, sales plans, and marketing/advertising promotions for training workshops.
➤ Created and implemented sales training programs.
➤ Analyzed sales promotion efforts and developed new strategies.
➤ Expanded client base, securing several key corporate accounts.
➤ Increased business by 20 percent during the first year.

Sales Trainer, 1993–1997
Sales Corporation of Tallahassee, Florida
➤ Organized and presented sales training seminars.

Midshipman, 1988–1993
U.S. Navy, Miami, Florida
➤ Served on Commanding and Executive Officers staff.
➤ Awarded Sailor of the Month and Quarter.

EDUCATION

Bachelor of Business Administration, NROTC, 1988
Memphis State University, Memphis, Tennessee

Awarded: Achievement, Human Relations Award; Special Award for Achievement; and Highest Award for Achievement

ACTIVITIES

➤ Chair, Membership and Marketing Committee, Atlanta Country Club, 2004–2005
➤ Member, City Country Club, 2000–2005
➤ Fundraising Team, Atlanta Performing Arts, 2002–2005

References Available on Request

SUSAN L. JEFFERS
2235 S.W. Hammond • Laramie, Wyoming 82057
(307) 555-9872 • susanjeffers@xxx.com

CAREER GOAL
Communications Director in a corporate environment

DEMONSTRATED SKILLS
• Experienced with marketing and public relations: developing marketing strategies and campaigns, dealing with sensitive issues with the news media, and developing and projecting an organization's most positive image.
• Ability to develop plans, goals, strategies, and timelines and to maintain schedules and analyze results of projects.
• Work independently and exercise sound judgment.
• Excellent communications skills, both in writing and in making public presentations to small and large groups on a variety of topics.
• Ability to work effectively with the public, elected officials, board and committee members, program operators, and staff in a teamwork environment.
• Experienced in grant writing and fundraising.
• Thorough knowledge of state and federal government operations and regulations affecting business in the state.
• Experienced with preparation and production of graphics materials, including brochures, newsletters, websites, and annual reports.
• Knowledge of newspaper advertising department practices in advertising sales, placement, and design.

PROFESSIONAL EXPERIENCE
Research Specialist, Public Relations Department, State of Wyoming
June 2004 to present

Advertising Sales, *Laramie Evening News*, Laramie, Wyoming
January 2002 to May 2004

Advertising Production, *Sheridan Sun*, Sheridan, Wyoming
August 1998 to November 2001

Advertising Intern, *Laramie Evening News*, Laramie, Wyoming
June to August 1998

EDUCATION
B.A. in Journalism/Advertising, University of Wyoming, Laramie, 1998
Won AASA award for design of print advertising campaign

References available on request

RAOUL HARMON

910 NE 223rd #937
Brooklyn, NY 11201
(718) 555-2909
raoulharmon@xxx.com

OBJECTIVE

A position in the promotions department of a publishing house

WORK EXPERIENCE

Customer Service Assistant, 2003–present, Academic Book Service, Inc., Brooklyn, NY

- Research problems with library book shipments using custom C-Basic database, searching both archived records and current orders with publishers.
- Prepare documentation for library book returns for credit, and reorder correct books when required.
- Contact publishers for price and availability information regarding library orders.
- Determine type of credit issued, securing evidence involving discrepancies with library orders and actual books received.

Book Purchasing Clerk and Sales and Promotion Assistant, 2000–2003, Blue Water Gallery and Shop, New York, NY

- Responsible for book ordering and stocking.
- Assisted with merchandising.
- Assisted with production of publicity materials (fliers, signs, posters, invitations).
- Responsible for customer service and sales.

Senior Editor, 1992–2000, Blackman East, Inc., Newark, NJ

- Proofread and compared academic and public libraries' Series Authority file records against Library of Congress Authority file to standardize catalogued records.
- Edited records and bibliographic files using Basic language on an IBM terminal.
- Researched problem heading and series updates.

EDUCATION

B.A. 1991, City College of New York, NY
Philosophy and Literature

References available upon request

❖ Arthur Lewis ❖

789 Harborough Street
Boston, MA 02169
(617) 555-8962
arthurlewis@xxx.com

❖ Objective

To find employment in a human services field that offers new challenges and opportunities and utilizes the experience, skills, and knowledge from nearly 20 years of increasing responsibility in the education field

❖ Strengths

Creativity	Ability to synthesize diverse ideas into coherent concepts, to think in new directions, and to assist others in more clearly stating their ideas and objectives
Tolerance	Ability to work with a diverse population and enjoy the interaction and challenges of diversity; essentially team-oriented and a "people" person
Assessment	Ability to employ various standard and nonstandard assessment processes as well as mature insight in the evaluation of programs and proposals
Writing	Ability to write informally and formally, imaginatively as well as in a scholarly, more research-directed style
Speaking	Ability to present challenging concepts in formal oral presentations; strong small group skills and experience; significant teaching ability with diverse student population

❖ Education

M.A., Education, 1993, University of Massachusetts, Boston, MA

B.A., African American Studies and American Literature, 1990, Boston University, Boston, MA

Page 1 of 2

❖ Employment History

Language Arts Department Head, Jamaica Plain High School
Jamaica Plain, MA. 2004–present.
Coordinate curriculum planning and implementation. Act as department liaison to school board and administration. Teach English, Creative Writing, Technical and Research Writing, American Literature, British Literature, and Multicultural Literature. Supervise the production and publication of a student literary magazine.

English and Writing Instructor, Jamaica Plain High School
Jamaica Plain, MA. 2000–2004.
Taught English, Creative Writing, Technical and Research Writing, American Literature, British Literature, Multicultural Literature, and Speech to high school students. Tutored remedial and advanced students of Literature and Writing. Served as faculty sponsor of African American Student Union.

Language Arts Instructor, Franklin Junior High School
West Roxbury, MA. 1995–2000.
Taught English, Reading, Speech, and Writing classes to 7th and 8th grade students. Faculty sponsor and advisor for the Student Drama Group.

Substitute Teacher, South Boston Districts
Boston, MA. 1993–1995.
Taught Language Arts classes in junior and senior high schools in South Boston.

References available on request

MARYANNE BARBARAS

38549 Palm Lane
Hialeah, Florida 33010
(305) 555-3088
maryannebarbaras@xxx.com

OBJECTIVE

To utilize proven skills in planning and managing programs and employees to help children's advocacy organization and manage its services.

EXPERIENCE

Manager, Customer Support, Peyton Products, Inc., Hialeah, Florida, 2001–present

MAJOR ACCOMPLISHMENTS

- Reorganized and combined the Manufacturing Order Service Department and Sales Customer Service Department into customer-sensitive customer support group.
- Developed procedures, systems, and a team concept to better utilize skills and talents while increasing productivity.
- Designed WORK program to promote a "quality of service" approach to customer relations.
- Coordinated the conversion of a new order system as well as participated in the formal design of the integrated sales/manufacturing system.
- Developed various inventory programs and systems to increase responsiveness to customer product requirements.
- Implemented programs designed to increase staff motivation to achieve positive growth through goal setting and recognition.
- Managed a staff of twenty professionals and nonprofessionals.

Manager, Order Service, Peyton Products, Inc., Hialeah, Florida, 1995–2001

MAJOR ACCOMPLISHMENTS

- Reorganized the three domestic and international order service product groups into one organization.
- Developed unifying procedures and a cooperative working environment.
- Developed closer interdepartmental alignment, improving production scheduling to meet customer product requirements.

MAJOR ACCOMPLISHMENTS *(continued)*

- Developed closer interdepartmental alignment with the customer service group to improve order/production status for improved customer relations.
- Increased staff development activity through conference attendance, advanced degree encouragement, and product group team leadership.

Customer Service Representative, Peyton Products, Inc, Hialeah, Florida, 1992–1995

Teacher, Lincoln Middle School, Tampa, Florida, 1986–1990

EDUCATION

- Columbia University Graduate School, September 1992
- Two-Week Seminar/Certification, Market Analysis for Competitive Advantage
- Florida State University, 1986
- Bachelor of Arts, History

REFERENCES AVAILABLE UPON REQUEST

JEAN HANAKA

3829 Deering Street, Apt. 23A • Portland, Maine 04101
(207) 555-2483 • jeanhanaka@xxx.com

Objective:

A position as staff photographer for a public relations firm or university communications department.

Education:

B.F.A., Photography, New England Institute of Art, Maine, 2004
Coursework in Art and Photography, South Central Community College, Buffalo, New York, 1986–1987
B.S., Liberal Studies, Plainfield College, Plainfield, Vermont, 1985

Professional Experience:

1997–present
Office Coordinator, Community Relations Office, University of Southern Maine, Portland, Maine

Produce educational and promotional material (copy and photos) for many campus events and displays, both on and off campus. Write advertising copy for both radio and newspapers. Design and assist in designing advertising layout for newspapers. Establish and reorganize procedures for maintaining records, billings, and follow-up; organize detailed record keeping for the Speaker's Service; initiate surveys and tabulation of area rental rooms, prices, and contact persons. Write office guidelines, including an office procedures manual. Maintain campus maps, staff directory, and new employee packets. Monitor and assign work to four classified staff and supervise three to six work-study students.

1994–1997
Senior Secretary, Community Relations Office, University of Southern Maine, Portland, Maine

Assisted the Community Relations Director. Maintained office records. Coordinated room reservations, Speakers' Service functions, and assignments for the Graphics area of the CRO.

1986–1994
Staff Photographer, Learning Resource Center, Buffalo, New York

Provided photographs for LRC newsletter, biannual bulletin, and promotion and publicity use. Researched community events, local news, and trends for news and photography leads. Attended all LRC events. Completed layouts of newsletter and bulletin.

Portfolio and references available upon request or online at jeanhanaka.com

Sandra B. Walters

334 Northwest Vineland Ave.
Concord, NH 03321
(603) 555-2214
sandrawalters@xxx.com

Career Interest:

Outward Bound Instructor in Mountain Climbing Division

Skills & Experience:

- First American woman to climb Tengeboche Himal in Nepal.
- Completed solo 1,000 mile trek in Chilean Andes.
- Made ascent to 21,000-foot elevation on Everest before weather ended expedition.
- Climbed seven major peaks in the Cascade Mountain Range in Oregon and Washington.
- Organized and led climbs to four major peaks in Rocky Mountains in Colorado and Wyoming.
- Organized and led treks on the Pacific Crest Trail from Canada to Mexico.
- Wrote book (as yet unpublished) on experience trekking in Third World countries.

Related Work Experience:

- Taught high school history in public schools for 12 years.
- Provided counseling assistance in program for drug-dependent youth.
- Taught short courses in backpacking and mountain climbing for local sporting goods store.
- Taught courses and led trips for university student outdoor recreation center.

Employment History:

History Teacher, South Concord High School, 2000 to 2005
History Teacher, Washington Lee High School, Boston, 1994 to 2000

Additional Work Experience:

Real Estate Sales, Central Home Realty, Boston, 1988 to 1994
Secretary, Central Home Realty, Boston, 1984 to 1988

Education:

Coursework in Counseling, University of New Hampshire, 1998 to 2004
B.A., History, Boston University, 1994

References available on request

• WANDA ELAINE FARBER •

14 East First Street • Wichita, Kansas 67231
(316) 555-6129 • wandafarber@xxx.com

• GOAL:

Develop a challenging career in sales leading to management in marketing and sales.

• PREVIOUS EXPERIENCE:

Office Manager, Martin Accounting, Inc., Wichita, Kansas, 2004–present
Handle all bookkeeping and office staff personnel responsibilities. Maintain payroll and ledger sheets. Monitor employee productivity and activity reports. Review actuarial expenditures and income periodically in accordance with budgeted figures. Work with owner to develop planning and financial reports.

Gift Shop Sales Clerk, St. Joseph's Hospital, Wichita, Kansas, 2002–2003
Responsible for stocking inventory, making and recording sales, balancing daily receipts, and closing gift shop after hours. Provided assistance to hospital visitors seeking gifts and greeting cards for patients. Responded to queries from nursing staff and doctors. Delivered floral bouquets as required.

Cashier, Wal-Mart, Wichita, Kansas, 1998–2002
Trained new employees on cashier's responsibilities and procedures. Made sales, recorded transactions, and balanced cash drawer at end of shift. Assisted with restocking. Answered questions for store patrons.

Childcare Provider, Little Ones Day Care Center (Self-Employed), Marquette, Iowa, 1988–1998
Started private day care center with two employees caring for 14 children, ages 18 months to 5 years. Developed and implemented preschool curriculum for older children. Provided informational newsletter to parents of children in the center.

• EDUCATION:

Continuing Education, Falls City, Community College, Wichita, Kansas
Completed 14 credit hours in Marketing through the Business Department; currently enrolled in Management Systems and Finance.

Associate Degree, Business, Central Community College, Cedar Rapids, Iowa
Coursework focused on business management, finance, and accounting.

References available on request.

STEPHAN MONETT

34 South Avon Street • Charleston, South Carolina 29411
(603) 555-2236 • stephenmonett@xxx.com

CAREER OBJECTIVE
Senior Manager leading to Project Director position

CAREER ACHIEVEMENTS
- Direct, supervise, and administer turnkey projects from inception to start-up for equipment manufacturing firm.
- Coordinate with sales department to review system process design, equipment, sizes, schedule, and engineering costs before presenting final proposal to the client.
- Negotiate purchases and advise corporate president and CEO of pending contracts and negotiations.
- Completed 17 domestic projects and 20 international projects in Latin America, South America, Spain, and Africa.
- Conceived, initiated, and successfully sold design of two new equipment products that resulted in a 40 percent increase in corporate sales over two years.
- Completed all projects on or ahead of schedule. All projects resulted in corporate profits; many produced higher profits than anticipated.
- Instituted procedures for project documentation handling and project communication.
- Trained project engineers and project managers to design and manage assigned projects.
- Instituted program for college interns and developed training program that culminated in job offers to those graduates whose performance met challenges of the position. After seven years, all students thus hired are still with the company and highly productive.
- Supervised four project management teams, including 12 engineers and 16 drafters.
- Acted as site project engineer during construction of $250 million plant.
- Registered professional engineer in the states of South Carolina and Arkansas.

CAREER EXPERIENCE
Senior Project Manager, DRG Inc.
Charleston, South Carolina, 1998–present

CAREER EXPERIENCE (continued)

Senior Project and Process Engineer, Hopewell Systems
Charleston, South Carolina, 1994–1998

Process and Plant Engineer, Toverston Dryers
Little Rock, Arkansas, 1991–1992

Pilot Plant and Process Development Engineer, James River Corporation
Neenah, Wisconsin, 1987–1991

EDUCATION

M.S., Chemical Engineering, Georgia Institute of Technology
Atlanta, 1998

B.S., Engineering, University of Wisconsin
Milwaukee, 1987

Professional References Available as Requested

Sample Cover Letters

This chapter contains sample cover letters for people pursuing a wide variety of jobs and careers.

There are many different styles of cover letters in terms of layout, level of formality, and presentation of information. These samples also represent people with varying amounts of education and work experience. Choose one cover letter or borrow elements from several different cover letters to help you construct your own.

15 March 20__

Human Resources
Director Search Committee: Senior Technical Editor
Merrick Engineering, Inc.
P.O. Box 223
Rutland, VT 05702

To the members of the Search Committee:

Enclosed is my application for the technical writer/editor position currently available at Merrick's Rutland office.

From the Environmental Computing Center to the new University Theatre and an endowed professorship in integrated circuit design, I have written, edited, and coordinated more than 150 grant proposals for many of the University of Vermont's most significant projects. As proposal writer for the University Foundation and Development Office, I work closely with vice presidents, deans, directors, and faculty to present their projects to both lay and technical audiences. I directly supervise two staff members and a student assistant, and coordinate the efforts of others involved in grant writing and fundraising processes within the University.

My graduate work in English and undergraduate studies in premedicine at Stanford have prepared me to write with ease on a variety of topics. I've edited complicated research presentations for many of the university's premier scientists while also working with leading scholars in the humanities to prepare fundraising documents for various cultural programs.

My experience as a freelance writer, graphic designer, and photographer further qualifies me for this position. Two of my recent publications present biographies and in-depth research abstracts on scientists featured in *Nobel Prize Winners: Physiology and Medicine*.

Your prospectus requested salary requirements. As my primary interest in the position is in the challenges it offers to put my skills to good use for a company that has a strong international reputation for excellence, I would be satisfied should the proposed remuneration meet my current gross annual income of $45,000, which includes salary and benefits.

I will be out of town until the 19th, after which I will be happy to meet with you. I would value the opportunity to join the strong and growing team at Merrick, and I appreciate your review of my application.

Sincerely,

Amada Wentworth

26 West Parade Drive * Rutland, VT 05702 * (802) 555-9847 * a.wentworth@xxx.com

TERRENCE WEST
4437 White Oaks Drive
Urbana, IL 61801
(309) 555-2847
terry.west@xxx.com

May 11, 20__

Mr. Arthur Davidson, Director
Davidson & Beckfield Associates
Suite 110, Ridley Tower
Chicago, IL 60621

Dear Mr. Davidson:

I was delighted to talk with you yesterday about your interest in hiring a public affairs director, and I want to restate my interest in learning more about the position.

So that you might learn more about my background, I have enclosed a summary resume for your review. If you prefer, I can forward my complete dossier, along with recommendations from professional associates.

What captures my interest about this position is the possibility for effecting change on a significant scale. My previous experiences have offered tremendous opportunity for influencing the country's growth in positive ways, but within fairly limited spheres: education and domestic economics, primarily. I have continued my involvement with social policy and public administration while lecturing at the university, and I am more convinced than ever that there is a great need for an organization like yours to turn its attention to unifying these issues in a direct and meaningful way. That is a challenge I would find immensely rewarding, both personally and professionally.

Our mutual friend, Helen Ashwood, told me I could find no more professional and respected an organization with which to align my efforts. After the discussion you and I shared this morning, I clearly agree with her astute assessment.

Therefore, I look forward to talking with you again soon.

Best regards,

Terrence West

Joseph W. Caldwell

346 Buena Vista • Pocatello, Idaho 83251
(208) 555-6682
josephcaldwell@xxx.com

February 21, 20__

Frank Martin
Jones Construction Co.
3356 Highway 36
Pocatello, Idaho 83251

Dear Mr. Martin:

I am writing to apply for the foreman's position listed in the Human Services Division Office. My resume is enclosed, listing my previous work experience.

For the past 7 years I have worked as the supervisor at Twin Peaks Plywood Mill, where I was responsible for 24 workers on a shift. I also scheduled workers for two other shifts. The closure of the mill has prompted my return to construction work, which I did successfully as a union carpenter for nearly 10 years.

I believe my construction background together with my supervisory experience provide the qualifications you are looking for in a construction foreman. I have worked on both single- and multiple-family housing as well as several-story office buildings, and I am familiar with building codes in Idaho as a result of building my own home.

I would like to call and make an appointment to talk with you, or you can reach me at 555-6682. Thank you for considering my application.

Sincerely,

Joseph W. Caldwell

Angelina Bergman

884 NW 12th Avenue
Fort Worth, Texas 76109
(214) 555-1985 (daytime)
(817) 555-9712 (evening and weekend)
angelabergman@xxx.com

March 21, 20__

Corrine Bracken, Executive Director
Design Engineering
20 West Tenth
Dallas, Texas 76443

Dear Ms. Bracken:

In reply to your advertisement in the March 15th *Wall Street Journal*, I am enclosing a professional resume and letters of recommendation for the position of Vice President of Sales and Marketing.

I believe the executive management positions I've held with DaMark-Dolin America have given me the experience and capabilities you are looking for in a top marketing executive. DaMark-Dolin has recently been acquired by InnaVail Corp., and I have chosen to seek new opportunities and challenges within the corporate management sphere.

I have taken the liberty of calling to arrange for an appointment to speak with you further in order that I might learn more about your expectations and how I might make a significant contribution toward Design Engineering's future progress and growth. Per your secretary, Mary Dolan, I'm planning on meeting with you on April 5 at 2 P.M. Please feel free to call or e-mail me if you have any questions in the meantime.

Best regards,

Angelina Bergman

DARIUS W. HARMS

3485 Plainfield Road

Lincoln, Nebraska 68573

(402) 555-9287

dariusharms@xxx.com

March 1, 20__

Jonathan Parker
Engineering Division Director
State of Nebraska
P.O. Box 5678
Lincoln, Nebraska 68570

Dear Mr. Parker:

Please accept this letter and the enclosed resume in application for the Engineering Supervisor position announced February 25.

I believe my extensive background in structural and mechanical engineering meets or exceeds the qualifications you are looking for. I have served both as a senior engineer and as an engineering supervisor with responsibility for 120 workers.

For my part, I would like to put my expertise and experience to work for the benefit of public works projects, where safety and quality form the guiding values, as stated in your position description. Too often in the corporate world, the demand for higher profit margins takes precedence over innovative developments and worker safety. My experience in this field, however, has given me the ability to achieve desired results in the most efficient manner possible, thus cutting costs and increasing productivity.

Please review the enclosed resume and call me at the number above. I would like very much to talk with you about the position and what my experience can bring to your department.

Sincerely,

Darius Harms

Samuel Hussad

131 Mountain Drive • Longmont, CO 80501
sam.hussad@xxx.com • (303) 555-2435

April 1, 20__

Susan Franklin
Personnel Director
Specialist Books
P.O. Box 2362
Denver, CO 80235

Dear Ms. Franklin:

Please accept the enclosed resume and letters of recommendation in application for the Senior Editor position with the Science & Technical Division of Specialist Books. I am responding to the position announcement listed in the March 26 edition of *Publishers Weekly*.

Currently I am managing editor of the University of Colorado Press, with full responsibility for acquisitions, development, design, and production. The position has been an extremely rewarding one, but statewide budget cuts within higher education have resulted in indefinite closure of the press. Therefore, I would like to put my energy and extensive publishing background to work for Specialist Books in your Science and Technical Division.

Approximately 65 percent of the titles I published with the UC Press were of a scientific or technical nature, and I gained additional editorial experience in the field as Editorial Assistant of the Environmental Studies Department of the university.

I would be happy to forward copies of relevant publications, both initial manuscripts and final publications, as examples of my editorial work. I would also appreciate an opportunity to discuss the position with you personally. I can be reached at the above number after hours and on weekends, or I can be reached via e-mail during the week.

I look forward to receiving your call and thank you in advance for your consideration.

Yours sincerely,

Samuel Hussad

GLORIA SANTOS
2534 Collins Avenue
Miami, Florida 33239
g.santos@xxx.com
(315) 555-8906

March 25, 20__

Pat Newton
Personnel Director
Lane Michaels Associates
345 Main Street
Miami, Florida 33219

Dear Ms. Newton:

In response to the March 18 advertisement for a Financial Resources Associate in the *Miami Herald*, I am submitting the enclosed resume and salary requirements for your consideration.

For the past 13 years, I have worked as an accountant and office manager for a variety of organizations. My interest in the financial resource management of these organizations led me to return to graduate school at the Florida International University for a certificate in financial management, which qualifies me as a financial resources counselor and securities adviser.

My coursework involved extensive study of economic theory, policy, and practice, as well as the specific methodologies of financial analysis and resource management. My previous experience as an accountant served me well in pursuing study in these areas, and I believe it has allowed me to bring a unique perspective to the analysis and management of finance.

I would like to meet with you to discuss the position and your requirements in more detail as well as present further support for my specific qualifications for the position. I am available at the number above any day after 2:00 P.M., and on weekends. I look forward to talking with you, and thank you for your consideration.

Sincerely,

Gloria Santos

SUNIL RAJAH
1233 Mission Street • San Pablo, CA 98329
(212) 555-0812 • s.rajah@xxx.com

January 20, 20__

Personnel Director
Bakersfield & Associates
Box 123
San Pablo, CA 98332

Dear Director:

Please accept the enclosed resume in application for the position of associate sales director, which was advertised in the *San Francisco Chronicle* last week.

After an interesting and rewarding career as an engineer, I returned to graduate school to pursue a growing interest in business, specifically in marketing and sales. Early in my career, I gained some valuable experience as the Engineering Sales Specialist for Shell Oil Company. In this position, I worked with manufacturers and small business owners to coordinate efforts for fuel efficiency and cost savings. The marketing and sales program that resulted was the most successful sales program in the company's history.

During my graduate program at Oregon State University, I worked closely with several faculty members in consultation with a major technology manufacturer in the area to recast the company's image and stimulate sales in a slow economy. The strategic planning sessions with corporate executives provided a tremendous on-the-job training opportunity for me as a graduate student, and the project achieved the desired results.

My inquiries have revealed that your firm has a strong reputation for excellence and innovation that makes me eager to bring my skills in strategic planning and market analysis to work for Bakersfield & Associates.

I would appreciate an opportunity to discuss the position with you further. Please call me at (212) 555-0812, where messages may be left if I am personally unavailable.

Thank you for your consideration.

Sincerely,

Sunil Rajah

Molly McShane
20876 Hopewell Avenue
Aurora, IL 60571
m.mcshane@xxx.com
(847) 555-3833

February 19, 20__

Andrew Martin
Executive Director
Sheraton Hotel
600 Shoreline Drive
Chicago, IL 60615

Dear Mr. Martin:

I am enclosing my resume and three letters of recommendation in reply to
the position announcement for Personnel Director at the Chicago Sheraton
Hotel.

I believe you will find that my experience has provided me with the qualifications you are looking for in your top personnel officer. I have held several
managerial positions with responsibility for personnel issues, including handling union negotiations and safety regulations. I am also well versed in
payroll accounting and the required quarterly tax reports.

As you will note from the enclosed letter from my current employer, David
Harris of Jordan Distributing, the downsizing of the corporate management
structure has left no clear path for advancement within the organization.
While I have enjoyed my tenure with Jordan, I am interested in taking on
new challenges, particularly in the area of personnel management.

Once you have reviewed the enclosed material, I would appreciate an
opportunity to talk with you further. I can be reached at 847-555-3833.
I look forward to talking with you.

Thank you for your consideration.

Sincerely,

Molly McShane

143 W. 19th • Everett, WA 98215

March 13, 20__

Mr. Jack Dunn
Superintendent
Everett School District
P.O. Box 16394
Everett, WA 98235

Dear Superintendent Dunn:

John Nukes in your department recommended that I write to you to express my interest in the Associate Principal position currently being advertised for the Everett Junior High School. Enclosed you will find a summary resume.

After several years with increasingly responsible positions in the Bethel School District in Alaska, I have returned to my hometown with the desire to continue my career in education administration. I believe my educational background and classroom and special programs experience give me the qualities needed to be a successful associate principal.

Most recently I was involved in a special project to develop an incentive program for boosting school attendance. The program brought together a broad base of community support and provided an opportunity for children to learn more about their own cultural backgrounds as well as that of others in the community. It was a tremendous success. At a time when educational support from taxpayers is faltering, it is imperative to develop timely, location-specific programs to get people involved in our schools. I look forward to the challenge of stimulating my hometown to greater public support for the school programs.

I will call your office early next week to schedule an appointment to speak with you further about the position and my qualifications. If you would like to reach me before then, I am available at (206) 555-9283. I look forward to meeting with you soon.

Sincerely,

Andrew Vizenor

Robert L. Dykstra
1854 S. Franklin Ave.
Grand Rapids, MI 48059
bob.dykstra@xxx.com
(616) 555-8376

January 19, 20__

Jane K. Shapiro
Director of Development
Art Exhibitors of Southwest Michigan
16 Bayshore Drive
South Haven, MI 48098

Dear Ms. Shapiro:

I am very interested in applying for the position of Communications Specialist in the Development Department. Enclosed are a brief summary and some samples of publications for which I have served as editor and designer.

As a member of the cultural scene in Grand Rapids for the past ten years, I have lately felt a need to get more directly involved in helping the arts continue to thrive, not just survive. Toward this end, I have recently begun looking for positions in which I could take an active role in arts support and advocacy. I believe my dedication as well as my skills in the communications media will serve the position profitably.

After you've had an opportunity to review the enclosed material, I would like to meet with you personally. I can be reached at the above number, or I will call you by the end of next week to schedule an appointment. I am eager to talk with you further about the position and how I envision my contribution to your organization.

Thank you for your consideration.

Sincerely,

Robert L. Dykstra

MAIA JOINER

24 Wellington Place • Tallahassee, FL 32311
maia.joiner@xxx.com • (904) 555-6787

January 16, 20__

Susan Winslow, Director
Public & Corporate Relations Department
Hammond, Powell, Hyde and Carter
24 W. Broadway, Suite 1215
Tallahassee, FL 32301

Dear Ms. Winslow:

Please accept this letter and the enclosed resume in application for the position of public relations associate for broadcast production currently open at Hammond, Powell, Hyde and Carter.

For the past 25 years, I have worked in the broadcast media industry and gained a wealth of knowledge of media affairs, public interests, and corporate communications. I believe the perspective I bring from my background on the "other side of the fence" will serve me well in your department.

My technical background in electronics and video technology have also proven invaluable when producing video programs and advertisements. With a thorough understanding of how such a program is made, I can use the medium to its best advantage.

I would like to show you some footage from several of the projects I have worked on, both recently as production engineer for the "Channel 5 News at Noon" and from my tenure as public relations associate for WJKE-FM Radio.

Thank you for your consideration. I look forward to hearing from you.

Sincerely yours,

Maia Joiner

❖ Arthur Lewis ❖

789 Harborough Street
Boston, Massachusetts 02169
(617) 555-8962
arthurlewis@xxx.com

February 21, 20___

Dr. Frank Parminter
Executive Director
Department of Health and Human Services
452 Center Street, Suite 3305
Boston, Massachusetts 02135

Dear Dr. Parminter:

Thank you for sending the information I requested concerning the Public Information Officer position currently available with your department. I would like to apply for the position. I am enclosing my resume, the requested letters of recommendation, and my salary requirements.

I can bring to this position some unique skills gained through several years as a language arts instructor in the high school system. Teaching writing and communication skills is perhaps the best possible way to expand and refine one's own skills as well as knowledge of production processes for printed publications.

I would like to have an opportunity to talk with you further about the position and the specific strengths I can bring to your department. I will call your office early next week to schedule an appointment at your convenience.

I look forward to meeting you and learning more about the program areas the department covers. Thank you for your kind attention.

Sincerely,

Arthur Lewis

Juanita Rodriguez-Sutton

330 Hollywood Boulevard • Los Angeles, California 90063
(213) 555-2475 days • (213) 555-0248 evenings • j-rodriguez-sutton@xxx.com

March 26, 20__

Jefferson Grant, Director
Hollywood Ad-Man
443 La Ciernica Boulevard
Hollywood, California 90028

Dear Jeff:

I enjoyed talking with you Thursday about the A.D. position with Hollywood Ad-Man. After our discussion, I came away convinced that I'm the woman for the job. Once you've reviewed the enclosed resume and agency list, I believe you'll agree.

You mentioned that one area not currently covered by staff members' experience is research and market analysis; you've had to contract this work out or rely on hunches and suppositions. I can bring extensive experience in both areas to take some of the guesswork out of strategic planning and target advertising.

I've also had significant experience with broadcast media, both radio and television. Given the trend in advertising today toward a reliance on cable television outlets, additional experience in this area could be a strong plus for your company.

I will call you next week to talk more about the job and what I can bring to the position. Again, I enjoyed our conversation and look forward to meeting with you soon.

Best regards,

Juanita Rodriguez-Sutton

KARL LI

290 Summit Drive
Portland, Oregon 97208
(503) 555-0709
karlli@xxx.com

April 16, 20__

Sibyl Jameson
Vice President, Marketing & Sales
Simmons & Wooster, Ltd.
21 Grand Street
Portland, Oregon 97210

Dear Ms. Jameson:

I was delighted to talk with you yesterday about the sales manager's position currently open at Simmons & Wooster. As you requested, I am forwarding a summary resume outlining my previous experience in the world of nonprofit corporation development. I have also enclosed some sample publications produced under my direction at both the Willamette Valley Health Care Foundation in Portland and the Children's Foundation in Chicago.

   In many ways, the worlds of fundraising and sales are very closely related. In both, one asks a potential patron to part with hard-earned income in exchange for some kind of return. With fundraising, my job was to persuade patrons of the value of such intangible returns as a lasting kindness or a tax deduction come April 15th. Marketing also plays an extremely important role in fundraising activities: presenting a strong corporate image, the need to keep the corporation in the public eye, and selling a potential donor on something as elusive as a concept.

   In my familiarity with the quality of the products and service provided by Simmons & Wooster, I can say with certainty that developing and directing sales campaigns will be both stimulating and rewarding. I am looking forward to our April 26 meeting so that we can further discuss your expectations for this position and how my background will allow me to bring some fresh insights to the role of sales manager.

With best regards,

Karl Li

FAITH NGUYEN

775 SW Tillbury Road • Fresno, CA 93723
(203) 555-7623 • faithnguyen@xxx.com

February 6, 20__

Ms. Ellen Carlson
Senior Director
California Department of Economic Development
One Government Plaza
Sacramento, CA 95813

Dear Ms. Carlson:

Thank you for the information you sent in regard to the Project Manager's position with the CDED. I would like to submit the enclosed application and resume for your further consideration.

I have worked with the Consortium of California Counties for several years, and I believe I have found my niche in the area of project management. I have handled a wide range of projects with increasing levels of managerial responsibility. Most recently, I directed the planning, coordination, and management of a major statewide conference on job training, which involved the participation of several international specialists. I was given less than two months to arrange the entire project, and yet the results received appreciative reviews from all participants.

After a long and rewarding tenure with the Consortium, however, I am aware that I have reached the extent of opportunities for advancement within the organization. Therefore, I am looking forward to new challenges, and would very much like to join the impressive program at CDED.

I can be reached by e-mail at faithnguyen@xxx.com or by phone at (209) 555-7623. I look forward to hearing from you and discussing how I might contribute to your program.

Sincerely,

Faith Nguyen

ABDUL RAHMAN
345 Coral View, Apt. 9B * Coral Gables, FL * 33128
(305) 555-7823 * abdulrahman@xxx.com

February 27, 20__

Personnel Director
Patterson Printing
Box 1263
Miami, FL 33551

Dear Sir or Madam:

I am writing to apply for the Production Manager position advertised in Sunday's edition of the *Miami News*. Enclosed is my resume and statement of salary requirements.

In my 25 years with the printing industry, I have worked primarily as a mechanical or operational engineer concerned with the technical end of printing machinery. More recently, I have developed an interest in and discovered a facility for managing the front end of the business: production and press preparation. As manager of Graphic Arts Engineering and the D.E.C. Printing Group, I took on increasing responsibility for the management and facilitation of the production processes in addition to the engineering concerns of the equipment. During my tenure in this position, I implemented programs that increased efficiency by approximately 35 percent and thus significantly increased the company's profit margins.

By concentrating my energies more fully on production management, I believe I can achieve significant gains for Patterson Printing as well. Once you have reviewed the enclosed material, I would like to talk to you further about your organization and how I might become a part of your team.

I look forward to hearing from you.

Sincerely,

Abdul Rahman

JONATHAN B. OWENS

2245 RIVER ROAD • NEWPORT, OR 97366

(503) 555-2435 • jonathanowens@xxx.com

31 March 20__

J. Paul Murky
Executive Director
Human Resources Consortium
State Office Complex, Suite 743 B
Salem, OR 97310

Dear Mr. Murky:

After 20 years of active duty in the U.S. Coast Guard, I am ready to move inland and take on new challenges in a civilian career in program development and implementation. I would like to bring my experience in training and curriculum development to work for you in the position of Management Specialist III. In response to the position announcement, I am submitting the enclosed application for your review.

My most recent responsibilities with the Coast Guard involved the development, design, and implementation of a curriculum for training Coast Guard personnel in emergency response and medical training. I was responsible for selecting and evaluating a staff of 35 for the Central Training Center. In addition, I established a new computer system to improve communications, which utilized electronic mail and enabled instant communications with Coast Guard facilities around the world.

I would like to speak with you personally about the position and my unique qualifications. Please call me at the number above, and I will be delighted to travel to Salem to meet with you at your convenience.

Thank you for your consideration. I look forward to talking with you.

Sincerely,

Jonathan B. Owens

Judd Riley, Jr.

P.O. Box 1254 • Sioux Falls, SD 57103 • (605) 555-3828 • juddriley@xxx.com

March 21, 20__

Public Relations Manager
Bryson Department Store
1289 Main Street
Sioux Falls, SD 57114

To the Public Relations Manager:

I would like to submit the enclosed resume for your consideration in hiring the next Customer Service Manager at Bryson. My experience in public relations, marketing, and sales combine to offer you more than the required qualifications listed in your position announcement.

As the Assistant Director for Public Relations at Morris Brothers, I worked closely with consumers who had purchased or were interested in learning more about our products. In cases of complaints from consumers, I quickly and efficiently determined the problem and achieved a solution that met both the consumers' needs and the corporation's goals.

In sales and marketing, I have worked on a variety of market research projects and coordinated targeted promotional campaigns. I have also held supervisory positions in both sales and public relations.

After you have reviewed the enclosed resume, I hope you will call me at 555-3828 so that we can discuss both your expectations and the qualities I can bring to the position. I look forward to an informative discussion.

Sincerely yours,

Judd Riley, Jr.